I Thank God That Big Mouth Bass Don't Talk, or Do They?

I Thank God That Big Mouth Bass Don't Talk, or Do They?

How to Live Your Faith-Based Life to Your Full Potential and Purpose in 26 Days!

T. C. Morgan

ISBN: 0692832408
ISBN 13: 9780692832400

WHY I WROTE THIS BOOK

HAVE YOU EVER wished you could re-wind the tape of your life to make a situation right, correct a mistake or to say, "I Thank God That Big Mouth Bass Don't Talk, Or Do They? Well, here is your second chance opportunity to be inspired, encouraged and share your experiences with the Bass family on "How to Live Your Faith-Based Life to Your Full Potential and Purpose in 26 days!"

YOU WILL SURVIVE the disappointments and challenges associated with everyday life. But you will thrive in Your faith-based life with the Gifts of Faith, Hope and Love. Each chapter is linked to a powerful biblical manifestation which is your daily prayer empowerment and biblical topic so worthy of a twenty-six (26) seconds meditation to welcome each day.

Afterwards, feel the excitement of self-empowerment each day for twenty-six (26) minutes. Be creative as you study each chapter. Your daily devotion affirms your daily scripture and confirms the path for your life, one day at a time. Afterwards, you will enjoy creating your journal entry to reflect a thought-provoking daily quote, poem or food for thought. Please share your journals with others to galvanize them to live and grow in a faith-based life!

Join me and my family all in the name of Faith, Hope and Love. You might just discover and recognize that life's challenges and disappointments are often disguised as "Gifts of Faith, Hope and Love."

Our Measure of Faith

(Picture Copyright 2016 protected)
The creation of Pink Lady Sassy Bass.

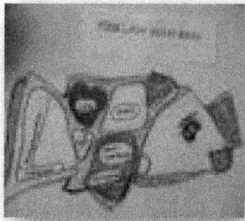

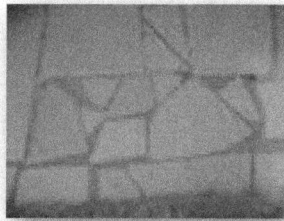

THIS ENTIRE FAITH-BASED romance, comedy and self-help book was written upon faith and led by hope, really.

I even asked God for the fish template sincerely.

I prayed in the bathroom one day and asked God for a prototype and looked down with a smile,

Glory to God there was Pink Lady Sassy Bass swimming in the bathroom tile!

DEDICATED TO MY MOTHER

My Beautiful Noir Madonna Speaks Faith to Heal (Holy Bible, Matthew 15:28)

THEN JESUS ANSWERED and said unto her, O woman, great *is* thy faith: be it unto thee even as Thou wilt. And her daughter was made whole from that very hour.

Many years ago, I was protected by her prayers sealed with tears locked into a bottle by God who cannot lie. (Psalms 56:8)

A Mother's prayers and her faith will cure her children and her loving spirit will never die.

Our Beloved Mother and her Unborn Son
The late, SARAH BELLE aka MY NOIR MADONNA and Son, DARIUS. "You gave us divine inspiration, your love of art, song and verse." We all have lived vicariously through your life gone way too soon. Your life has been amazing in such a short time and we honor

your plight to make a difference in the world. You have always left people better than you found them. Your life was an open book. For that reason, we remember you as the 67th "Book of Sarah" **as if it were written in the Holy Bible the Lamb's book of Life.**

Love, Your Children
Lynne, Alesia, LaCara and Ray

FAITH-BASED HAPPY BIRTHDAY LULLABY (SONG: 1 OF 3)

By T. Cobb Morgan, Lizgirl58@gmail.com

Happy Birthday, Happy Birthday, remember to keep the faith.
Promote peace and love and stand in HIS grace,
Singing Happy Birthday, Happy Birthday, Hold on to your dreams,
Glory in your suffering and find out what it means,
Grow in Perseverance and Character and Hope always,
He will bless your spirit to see better days.

(Song: 2 of 3) Promote peace and love and stand in HIS grace,
Singing Happy Birthday, Happy Birthday, Hold on to your dreams,
Glory in your suffering and find out what it means,
Grow in Perseverance and Character and Hope always,
He will bless your spirit to see better days.
Singing Happy Birthday, Happy Birthday,
Romans 5:1- 5, Your joyful soul will forever stay alive,
Happy Birthday, Happy Birthday, help me sing and come along,
so that (Song: 3 of 3)   You and well wishers will be blessed with love and a Birthday Song and a Birthday Song.

TABLE OF CONTENTS

Ask the Father in My Name…

²³And in that day ye shall ask me nothing. Verily, verily, I say unto you, whatsoever ye shall ask the Father in my name, he will give *it* you. ²⁴Hitherto have ye asked nothing in my name: ask, and ye shall receive, that your joy may be full.

John 16:23-24

PART 1

1

ASK GOD WHY?
WJF- Ask God Why?

To have a great untold story is confining,
To tell a great story is serendipity unwinding!

TERRY COBB MORGAN

Subtitles in
Chapter One

A Blackberry Rose Letter Ensures We are Friends.
Goodbye Earl, I'm Going Forward , Darkness Now Ends.
Memories are Not for Sale, You Must Give Them Away.
Dear Lizzie, Don't Smoke, George Burns has Jokes Today!
A Song Soothes the Body, Soul and Spirit to Last.
Renew, Refresh and Rebuild ; Relax to Heal it !
Check His Eyes, They hold Lies and Disguise
When the Soul Hurts.Pray and Be Wise

BlackBerry Rose Letter 26

Dear Beloved,

How are you? I pray all is well. I thank you for taking the time to read my letter and book... I am humbled and overjoyed with your response. Here are several relevant reasons why I chose to surround my message around the power of number twenty-six (26).

The Blackberry Rose Letter 26 and plan is powerful and as easy as ABC. There are Twenty-six 26 manifestations for letters A-Z along with care messages for encouragement.

Beloved, Believed and Praised" are noted 26 times in the bible of Christian love. I extend wisdom and love to you either as a fragrant velvety rose (female) or a deep sweet juicy blackberry (male) going through your prickly-stem stage of life, not realizing the awesome beauty of your God given anointed purpose and full potential.

I invite you to join me as we journey to "The Beginning, of the living land of The Garden of Eden. God is known as the respected and revered "Trinity" (3), The Father, The Son and The Holy Spirit. GOD created us in their image. In Genesis 1:26, it states: Then God said, Let <u>Us</u> make man, Adam and Eve,<u> image</u>, according <u>to Our likeness</u>; let them have dominion over the fish of the sea, over the birds of the air, and over the cattle, over all the earth and over every creeping thing that creeps on the earth.

Genesis 1:26.

In Greek, the relevant number, 26, is agape meaning divine love which represents God. In a perfect world, the "Trinity" exists comfortably in the family bible displayed on our living room table and safely tucked away.

I too am "safely tucked away" in my creature of habit predictability, weak pious state of mind and wavering character. That is, until the three of them found me in my less than perfect world crying on the Hampton Roads Bridge and my right arm shook uncontrollably. Why was it shaking? I was not hungry. I didn't feel nervous. But I was locked away in a terrible funk… it was so sad. From that day to this, I thanked God for a second chance and forgiveness, "for his mercy endureth forever" is noted twenty-six (26) times in Songs of Songs (Solomon) in the bible.) My prayer is that you are reading this faith-based book because it is a blessing just for you and not to you. Some have found it be a "gift of hope" and have made my biggest dream to serve the world come true! Please share the blessing to help others to receive a "gift of hope."

I thank you with heartfelt expression and ask you to speak continued blessings upon yourself and others you meet along the way. Give God the glory, choose to have a good day and smile at life!

Good-bye Earl

GOOD-BYE AND GOOD riddance," I said to Earl, a name which I gave to my last dark day. Finally, it is time to close a dark hole of daunting images echoing my soul and haunting a broken, ugly and leaking past.

I refuse to give them any further refuge in *my* existence. They have cursed generations of Bass Family souls prior to my birth. However, before my death, I must tell my story to end future generational curses and recreate a legacy of favored blessings. There will be unmerited portions of love and undeserving grace for me, my family, friends and even you. But, if we continue to think only to save ourselves we will continue to precede and follow another lost generation. We also lose the compassion to help one another and without notice, we will lose the true passion of our life ministry… and w*hen the darkness of Death hovers, we will have no compassion or legacy; will walk expressionless, cold and stiff as zombies to our coffins and simply climb in for an eternity of unrest.*

My initial mission, my dream and my message of hope was to serve as an advocate to those individuals suffering an illness, injury or disease which has mushroomed into a disability of lost hope and fallen-down despair. However, my friends enjoyed the 26 days of faith-based living so much they encouraged me to give an opportunity to all. Thank-you… point taken! Therefore, let's begin a spiritual stretch to REBUILD your body, REFRESH your spirit and RENEW your soul. I pass the baton, "not TO you, but FOR you" to run your life marathon past the competitors of haters, closed doors and no's. Be sure to thank them with determination, perseverance and anchor leg speed to win your fullest potential … with joy!

The River Cried a Million Tears,

As Love Crosses All Barriers
As a Child, I trusted God and the river to catch me
when I jumped into its warm water wave-like arms,
Sharing the space with a friendly seaweed eating turtle,
she flaunted her gold shell of nature printed charms.

I loved the river, hot Virginia summers and how
the swimmers crossed ALL barriers in the name
of a Sunday afternoon day at the beach,
Didn't they understand anything earlier the Pastor had
preached especially the crying river unleashed?

I guess we grow up to form opinions about others we fear
for not looking like us but God declared it from above,
If we are ever to see His face, it will probably-
Reflect the ultimate diversity of mankind, we must
start NOW accepting one another in love.

My Faith-Based Life as a Child Taught Me to LOVE

To completely embrace the 26 (twenty-six) day faith-
based plan and how it nourishes your Body, Soul and
Spirit we must understand their dynamics pool,
I may have gone too far back to my earliest knowledge of being a three part entity in Sister Emily's Sunday
school class. She taught, we all represent three enti-
ties which I refer to as the "Hero of the Trio." That
means we were born with a natural body, a soul and a
spirit which is a little confusing to a second grader.
She approached my desk and leaned down to me with
her large expressive eyes and waist length hair she kept
neatly in a in a bun covered by a white hair net.

Lizzie, hold out your hand" she requested. "What did I do?" Was she
going to spank my hand for asking a question? She looked at my hand
and ring that I begged my mother for in the bubble gum machine at
GEX, a sixties Walmart.

She said, "Your ring is pretty and God knew you would be wearing it at this appointed time. Lizzie, no matter what you're going through in life, happy or sad, always know that God loves you and so do I. All three parts,

Gee, I Never had a "STRANGER" tell me they loved me before. In fact, I never had anyone outside of my family, tell me they loved me and back then it was used sparingly.

Love! I thought it was really cool to say that groovy soap opera word during the 1960's. There was so much unrest and tension among the races during that time when segregation was ending.

Our parents shielded incidents from us as much as they could. I remember our family receiving an invitation from another great couple at the church, the Godshelleys. They were a model Faith-based family who lived the "Hero of the Trio" name I use when discussing three parts of mankind. which is the Body, Soul and Spirit of a person in the name of Passionate Worship. In fact, our Pastor at that time would take a family out to dinner the first of each month by drawing names at the end of the service.

They showed "Radical Hospitality" on their own and welcomed us for family dinner. They planned a whole day of faith-based activities that would satisfy the whole being of the Natural Person: sustained by hearing, touching, tasting, smelling and seeing. (Dinner was provided.)

The Soul Person consists mind, will and emotions (Fellowship of games, swimming and genuine conversation was provided.)

The Spirit man is our spirit (strengthening our spirit to connect with the Holy Spirit)

Gather at the table all, it's time for supper. I ate sister Kartha's food like there was no tomorrow. The family's stunning brick rancher home was nestled on several acres of land with a picturesque view of the river.

Entering the foyer, it led to the dining area as the window curtains fanned breezes from the river all around the room making me shiver!

A sturdy walnut table adorned a pressed, white lace tablecloth which presented a smorgasbord feast in fussy hunter green, white and gold Ming dynasty china. I stared at the intricate design.

It certainly upstaged our A&P green stamp collection at home. We were welcome to "partake in this feast for the nourishment of our bodies." Brother Bernie's prayer chimed.

I would bow further and smell the feast of sliced roasted turkey, tender peppered roast beef and clove pineapple ham. Surrounding dishes were fresh tossed salad, gelatin ambrosia salad, red potatoes in green beans smelled delightful.

This was my first sampling of sweet and sour fruit chutneys and whole berry cranberry sauce. I couldn't wait to grab the sweet buttered homemade roll at the end of the basket I was ready to fight for and wash it down with mint Lemon iced tea. As the dinner opera meal presentation symphonized I wanted to stand and applaud.,

The Lemon Coconut cake and Bubbling Peach Blackberry cobbler teased my anticipation as they were placed on the table early, for their big debut.

My Eyes were big as saucers when their twin teen-age boys brought in a heavy ice cream churn filled with thick, frozen French Vanilla and ice. I stood and all agreed with a hand clapping Bravo!

Afterwards, all the children played a game to settle our food to prevent cramps. We ran to the River to dip into the warm July weathered water. How calming and therapeutic it felt.

I loved that river, hot Virginia summers and how faith-based living crosses ALL barriers in the name of LOVE. my heart melts.

My Faith-Based Life as a Teen-ager Gave Me Hope

During The following summer, we packed up the green and gold church van and went on a youth camp retreat to Goshen, Indiana. We witnessed a person confessing that she harbored an evil spirit. The youth leader warned others that evil spirits can transfer to other souls if they are not right with God.

Taking no chances, our group ran to our dorm rooms "to get right with God." We sat up all night reciting the prayer of salvation, James 4:7 "Submit therefore to God, resist the devil (evil spirits) and he will flee from you."

Today, I am no longer a Mennonite practicing member. However, I will never forget my loving roots from Calvary. By the way, I still look for Sister Kantha's fussy china pattern in hopes of getting a formal pattern number. Oh well, just like my Monday diet, which ends by Wednesday, I am sure it's discontinued.

Memories for Sale

During my twenties, I would occasionally take a Sunday ride to the river by the Godshelley's home. As I approached the long driveway of their home, I couldn't believe what I was seeing, as a large moving rental truck passed by me. I looked over again and saw the Realty sign, the home was for sale! I pulled over near the curb and noticed a box of Knick knacks by a trash pile. I curiously bent down to examine the contents. Wrapped in a lace tablecloth was Sister Kartha's Ming Dynasty china set! May I help you young lady? Startled, I got up and turned around. It was Sister Kartha with her soft eyes, matte white skin and "shy Di" smile! We hugged and I expressed sadness that she was leaving. She smiled. I asked her to sell the set to me. "Oh, no dear, memories aren't for sale. My face dropped as she finished. Lizzie, always remember, precious memories must be shared and given away! I thanked her for the childhood memories and for her kindness. "Enjoy the china set, use it to God's glory, to please the "Trinity (Father, Son and the Holy Ghost. We are also a trinity so be sure to serve food to the natural person, fellowship with the soul of a person and pray with spiritual person.

"Hey lady you're blocking the driveway," said the truck driver. "No problem," as I quickly put my box in the trunk and returned to say good-bye to Sister Kartha, but she was gone. I looked at the truck driver and asked him where did Mrs. Godshelley go?

MRS.GODSHELLEY? You mean Kartha, my older sister? Haven't you heard? "No sir," "heard what?" She died in her sleep from a blood clot five years ago.

<u>Dear Lizzie, don't smoke!</u>
My Faith-Based Life as a Young Adult Taught Me to Rely on Faith.

I had other encounters years later to support my spiritual experiences, collection of knowledge and wisdom from others. Eager to see the world, I flew to Chicago and became a flight attendant. I was working a flight to Los Angeles and had a pleasant conversation with George Burns. How ironic, while chewing on a huge cigar, he autographed my napkin, "Dear Liz, don't smoke!"

As we descended for landing I sat on the jump seat. I closed my eyes and smiled as I imagined George Burns was the huge Boeing 747 in animation with his huge round Ben Franklin style framed glasses over the nose of the jet. His comedic look and funny bone clarity inspired me to illustrate a depiction of the body, soul and spirit we all have and knew they were designed to soar in our existence. I'm going to describe them in flight terms as they interconnect. The Soul is comprised of your mind, will and emotions. What is the soul? It's that "Little Black Box" instilled in you which has recorded EVERYTHING during the flight of your life.

By the way, you can't destroy it, can't de-program it and God will need it back. It will endure and outlive your natural body controlled by seeing, tasting, touching, smelling and hearing.

Then there is the spirit of the pilot flying high and should there be in change in the flight plan, "God's autopilot button – the Holy spirit" takes over which yearns to keep your existence "flying high" to reconnect with Him.

Daniel 9:21-22 *...WHILE I WAS STILL IN PRAYER,* Gabriel, *THE MAN I HAD SEEN IN THE EARLIER VISION, COME TO ME IN SWIFT FLIGHT ABOUT THE TIME OF THE EVENING SACRIFICE. COME TO GIVE YOU INSIGHT AND UNDERSTANDING.*

Please don't forget to check your spiritual baggage. Would you like a fluffy pillow and a warm blanket? The Comforter, His Holy Spirit, will sustain you through the storms of life, cure your spiritual fear of flying and teach you how to navigate and relax during times of strife.

On your next flight of spiritual turbulence, call Him and you will feel His presence so near and you will be blessed and assured of a smooth landing in Him minus the fear.

Song: Soothe Your Body, Soul and Spirit

Narrative: I believe that our Mind, Will and Emotions make up
the Soul which is for God- all contained.
When your life is over your natural body will refrain. The Spirit
will soar to its destination like a plane.
And the Soul will come forth as God demands to tell your story
as He Searches the Lamb's book of life for your name.
(Hums)… then… Song Starts,
Who brought me here, what brought me here today
How did I get here, why did I get to stay?
Why am I crying, for mercy and for grace?
I need some answers, I need them here today
Where is my strength and who is my shield?
Who can I trust, I need some help right here
I lost all my joy and my heart has no song,
Don't know who to run to, don't know where to belong.
Then I heard David lift praises all to God,
For He heard my mercy cry and song,
Generational curses will be destroyed this way,
Salvation is the answer, believe in me,
You and your household will from this day will be free.
He gives us unconditional love, joy and peace.
Who brought me here, who brought me here today?
How did I get here, why did I get to stay?
Why am I crying, for mercy and for grace?
I need some answers and I need them here today
Where is my strength and who is my shield?
Who can I trust, I need some help right here
I lost all my joy and my heart has no song,
Then I heard David lift praises all to God,

For He heard my mercy cry and song,
Speak, Questions from the Soul
I believe that Mind, Will and Emotions make up the Soul all contained,
And when your life is over and your physical body is gone, they will spiritually remain.
Acts 16:31English Standard Version (ESV)
[31] And they said, "Believe in the Lord Jesus, and you will be saved, you and your household."
End of song by T. Cobb—LizLL03@aol.com

Refresh, Rebuild and Rejoice!

My Faith-Based Life as a Middle-age Adult

This is the day that the Lord has made and I will rejoice and be glad in it.

Wow, I feel rested today as I apply the last of my oatmeal facial mask. My cucumber covered eyes will not search eagerly throughout the dark bedroom for images and they will relax. I can feel the sun's rays filtering through the window blinds and mingling with the intervals of warm air steaming from the floor radiator.

The old radiator has whistled steams of comfort to me through years of childhood fears of sleeping in the dark, sleepless nights and now, cold anxiety which seems to be withering away as my creamy facial dries to a mild film of coconut cream and banana silk.

I am patiently waiting for the mail courier to pick up my screenplay. By the way, where are my markers to write the musical notes I hear in my head? I believe I am feeling a little anxious as a million other thoughts rush through my mind.

Knock! Knock!

There is the anticipated knock on the door. Did I really hear it? The courier will arrive soon to pick up my package.

I hear the birds chirping for me to relax and in unison as if to sing, "Fill our bowl Liz with fruit and seed and the Lord indeed has blessed another day. Tomorrow we give no thought because He always makes a way.

I see the other distraction in the yard... The community bird feeder is being guarded by Poppa Blue Jay, the Bully bird in the yard. His mate, "Girlie Blue" is up in arms because Lady JA JA, Aunt Irene's cat, is getting too close to her nest. If I could only speak "Bird" I'd tweet her an informal message stating that feline buxom boogey cat wouldn't dare climb a tree and mess up freshly painted Persian Pink claws nor would she risk a scratch to her diamond studded I.D. Collar.

Check His Eyes!

The fragrant "Virginia Girl" peaches smell so good! Looking out my window, I can hear the going on of the orchard customers across the grove. I loved those huge peaches when I was a little girl. I remember a snaggle-toothed childhood bite of the sweet succulent peach as the sticky nectar ran down my skinny arms. How delightful these peaches continue to satisfy the Bass family throughout the generations and they still bless my family's table. If peaches can endure generational curses of disease, pestilence and integration of hybrid seeds, then why can't my family? Today, my husband, MG will bake a fresh peach cobbler for our son, River, at his engagement party.

"Wait a minute," as I sashed the window down I see my husband MG across the street talking to a nice-looking unfamiliar woman on his weekly orchard run.

He has a bag of peaches in his hand and a seedless watermelon under the other arm. The woman places a small piece of paper in his shirt pocket. "Geez, did she offer MG her phone number? More importantly, why would he accept it?"

(Song☺ Check His Eyes. By T. C. Morgan – LizLL03@aol.com

Check his eyes, and you will see,
Check his eyes, if he is into you emotionally
Check his eyes! The windows to his soul are a dead - giveaway.
Check his eyes! for a lie or temptation to sway.
Men are cursed with the "Bad boy stare."
Says they're just looking" but they want and glare.
Check his eyes look in her direction,
Check his eyes, steals a glance in two seconds, easy as pie" they say,
He snaps back in place, four seconds, no delay,
Check his eyes, five seconds adjusts his shades
Hums a tune to a great day!

I can hear Grannie Hog Maw's voice again, she says, "Lizzy Turn in your Gladys Cravats (Bewitched) badge and get a life!." you are too old to be micro managing a man being a man." Grannie Hog Maw would say, "Child, flick off that man stress like an annoying booger before an interview. Now close your eyes as the soothing sun warms your eyelids and tell the good people your story.

Liz Tells Her Story – My Soul Hurts
Hello, I am Liz Bass…and I am a Parkinson's survivor who wanted to end it all. No, I am not talking about death as that was neither an option nor the answer I was seeking. I wanted to end it all with "preachy" and "religious" Christian friends *and family* who judged me behind my back with other "self-righteous pious bible carrying, scripture quoting, church shouting hypocrites who tried to convince me I did something wrong. Some even clued in digs of characters like Falcon Fate, Karma's an Itch! and hinted that perhaps Shala Sin was in my life. The sight of them and their spiteful old wives patched up tales, customized and

conjured up made my "soul" hurt. My mind was clouded, my will faded and my emotions became stoic.

Hello, anybody out there listening? We ALL have sin in our lives! I fell under a dark cloud of depression which rained on me five years as I hid from the world. I gained a negative spirit, a broken heart of self-pity and fifty pounds. My bible became too heavy, scriptures fogged my mind, and the loud glory hallelujahs dwindled down to whispers of amen. I ignored the Sunday morning crew's conference call ringing me on Monday morning to gossip. I didn't even care how short Sis. Sexy Sheena's dress was when her robe split open in the front of Pastor Powhatan 's pulpit during the choir's rendition of "He's Really, Really Been Good."

The only thing I had left was Hopeful Hope. Thank God there was no peanut butter in my room when Hopeful Hope came along. I would have spread on the desperation of emotional eating and devoured her too!

One morning I saw a little eye in the crack of my bedroom door. The Parkinson drugs gave me so many hallucinations; I just added "the eye" to the list. "Nana, may I come in"? It was my seven-year old grandson. As I turned around my scary cucumber and yogurt mask provoked a scream from both of us! Then we laughed. He looked at me and grinned, "Nana you know I'm older and not afraid of your beauty masks anymore. She replied, I know baby and I'm getting too old to think these masks are making me beautiful. He said, you are beautiful and I love you Nana, and I want to pray for you to be healed. He said, Dear God, I love you and are you having a good day today? My tears would not stop. My baby asked Almighty GOD, the KING of kings and LORD of lords" how was HIS day...in LOVE! Since that day my suffering has ended.

Yes, I still have aches and pains occasionally but without the suffering. God removed the disabling pain and cured me with enabling joy.

As your renewed faith-based believer "judgement-free" friend, I ask you in love, to tell me, which disability "survivor" are you and what are your options? In other words, who, what, when, where and why caused you to stumble upon your fork in the road? Did it warrant you to suffer? Did you struggle with despair as your faith dwindled down to the size of a tiny little mustard seed? Perhaps, you or a loved one remain feeling broken, ugly and leaking all over the place! Great!

This book is for you! Your secret is out and it is safe with me. Now, let's trash it in the bin with guilt, shame and vulnerability of a wounded spirit which can only lead to further dreadfulness.

Let's agree to a 26 Days Trial Run of a Faith Based Life and get back on track with five easy steps to a smarter, sexier, saner, savvy and successful you! Yes, God will honor the desires of your heart.

He promised in Psalms 37: 3-5.

3   Trust in the LORD and do good;
     dwell in the land and cultivate faithfulness.
4   Delight yourself in the LORD;
     And He will give you the desires of your heart.
5   commit your way to the LORD,
     Trust also in Him, and He will do it."

But, you must be willing to change your thinking and listen to the echoes of your inner child, which is your spiritual self and ask God "WHY?" Remember that tiny bit of faith you have leftover? Well that justifies you to ask God "Why".

In fact, He wants us to ask Him "Why?" Again, I must reiterate that tiny bit of faith puts us in the presence of His grace and glory. God reveals to us we are living the biblical Romans 5: 1-5. We are to glory in our suffering because suffering produces perseverance; perseverance, character; and character, hope. Hope with God love, reveals our purpose and open doors! Listen, our door is opening now.

Open the Door and Start Your Faith- Based Walk, Now!

A knock finally taps the door and Liz responds, "Come in." the door creaks as it opens slowly. The silhouette of footsteps slowly advances across the wooden floor toward the bed. Liz raises her arm and beckons no further.

Please don't let my mask frighten you. Simply nod your head "Yes" or "No". Are you alone? The Mail Courier nods, yes. Were you followed here? Mail Courier nods no.

Liz explains the Document is highly classified, Top Secret and Confidential information. You are to share it with no one. Do you understand? The Mail Courier nods yes. Liz purred, Perfect. Transportation will be waiting for you downstairs and will escort you to the drop off point and return. Wait there for further instructions.

The Mail Courier leaves and she is none other than four-year old Milani. She appears on front step "incognito" with a scarf on her head tied at the chin and sunglasses and play clothes. Her seven-year-old cousin, Pond, picks her up in a wagon tied to the back of his bike.

They travel ten feet to mailbox and drop off the thick envelope and return to front porch.

Yes, my courier is only four years old with strong "Big Milan" attitude and faith that she WILL deliver that package, I invite your "inward echoing four-year old faithful self" to stay and meet my family.

Pink Lives Matter – Meet Grannie Hog Maw!

Knock! Knock! Who is it?

Liz, its Grannie Hog Maw! I need to come in.

Sorry, Grannie Hog Maw I'm taping now.

I know that. Snort, Snort! What the Smell? (This is Grannie Hog Maw's phrase meaning "What is going on?") She pushes the door open and talks into the microphone) is this microphone on?

Hello, testing 1-2-3. Hello out there. This is your Grannie Hog Maw and I want you to meet the Bass Family Clan here in Virginia! I promise you upon meeting my zany, reasonably dysfunctional; loving family you will feel right at home!

Therefore, please feel welcome to stay and have a wonderful time! You will laugh, cry, play, eat some of my good food, sing and dance with the Bass family. Oh, by the way your secrets will remain safe with us because "I Thank God That Big Mouth Bass Don't Talk, (laughs) Or Do They?

Mural at the Top of the Stairs

I painted a mural at the top of the stairs,
Praying my weakened legs could make it up there.
I painted books to read and take me away,
There's a clock for time and a candle to light the way.
I see a lamp is there with a bright shine,
Reflects my faith to stay on this climb,
A duck makes me smile because I have duck feet!
A bowl of the Fruit of the Spirit with plenty to eat a drink from
husband's masonic cup, tonic water, neat
There is my son's 12-year-old Golden Retriever "puppy" saying,
you can make it Mom just stay on course,
God is everything…and HE is your source!
BY T. COBB MORGAN, lizgirl58@gmail.com ©

STOP! To Work on WJF: Worksheet, Journal REFLECT & FOCUS at the end of each chapter or CONTINUE.
<u>Manifestation End of Chapter One</u>
WJF - ASK GOD WHY?

Prayer: Pray for 26 seconds on topic of Focus- Biblical Manifestation: ASK GOD WHY?

Devotion" SCRIPTURE (John 16:23 - 29) Question/Comment/ Answer
ASK GOD WHY?!

Question: Will God be angry at me for asking Him "why" and is it biblically sound that I ask God, Why?

Answer: No, God will not be angry, He loves you. Yes! He wants you to know the plan He has for your life.

<u>Supporting Scripture:</u>
[23]And in that day ye shall ask me nothing. Verily, verily, I say unto you, whatsoever ye shall ask the Father in my name, he will give *it* you. [24]Hitherto have ye asked nothing in my name: ask, and ye shall receive, that your joy may be full. [25]These things have I spoken unto you in proverbs: but the time cometh, when I shall no more speak unto you in proverbs, but I shall shew you plainly of the Father. [26]At that day ye shall ask in my name: and I say not unto you, that I will pray the Father for you: [27]For the Father himself loveth you, because ye have loved me, and have believed that I came out from God. [28]I came forth from the FATHER and am come into the world: again, I leave the world, and go to the Father. [29]His disciples said unto him, Lo, now speakest thou plainly, and speakest no proverb.

John 16:23-29 & 26key verse

Devotion: You may also form a Lunch, Church or Sunday school study group to study a chapter for each session.

Journalize and Polish Your Purpose on Restoration: Read Psalms 23. Reflect on what you learned yesterday, today and give hope to tomorrow. Bring out your inner coloring kid and be creative! Color with crayons, coloring pens, pencils, highlighters and makers on the 23rd Psalm. Tape it to bathroom mirror and commit to memory.

Fish Hook Quote:
Better to ask God His Plan for your life, then to stumble and fall upon it through a lifetime of STRIFE! – T. Cobb-Morgan

BONUS EXERCISE - Assessing and Caring for the Soul

Key Scripture: Psalm 23: 1-6.

Challenge Question One: Read Psalm 23:1-6 below.
23 The Lord is <u>YOUR NAME</u> shepherd; I shall not want.2 He maketh me to lie down in green pastures: he leadeth me beside the still waters.
3 He restoreth my soul: he leadeth me in the paths of righteousness for his name's sake.
4 Yea, though I walk through the valley of the shadow of death, I will fear no evil: for thou art with me; thy rod and thy staff they comfort 5 Thou preparest a table before me in the presence of mine enemies: thou anointest my head with oil; my cup runneth over.
6 Surely goodness and mercy shall follow me all the days of my life: and I will dwell in the house of the Lord forever.

Diagnosis versus Prognosis

2

THE FIRST CUT IS THE DEEPEST
WJF- Diagnosis versus Prognosis

H ER EYES WERE fixed on the ceiling as he firmly pressed her throat in his hands. She prayed inside, Oh God please help me as she glanced at her husband's stoic facial expression for a few **seconds.**

She could feel her throat drying as a tear escaped her lower eyelid and slid down to her lip. It was as salty and bitter as her current situation.

She opened her eyes and squeezed out words in desperation, "Leumas, please let go."

Liz, are you okay? said Dr. Jefferson releasing his fingers from her throat. Your neck feels normal, but there is a little swelling in the back, a possible stoop developing, right hand tremor and a shuffling gait.

"LEUMAS, what would you say is my diagnosis?"

This visit was nothing like their previous General Practitioner visits. MG and Liz arrived at Dr. Jefferson's, office for an evening visit looking tired and worried. What happened? Life happened.

MG and Liz Bass are a middle aged, middle class married couple. They are at Liz's medical appointment. She has not been feeling well.

The successful Doctor Jefferson just examined her. MG is very concerned about his wife of thirty years.

She studied his face for the mysterious pause and what should have been a "quicker" response but it did not come. Dr. LEUMAS Jefferson, tall, soft spoken with salt and pepper good looks, wore expensive mint leaf cologne to mask his cigar smoke from his patients and especially his wife. He realized he had been their primary care physician for years, a family benefit they enjoyed since he is married to Liz' sister, LaCara.

He looked at both with special care…his family. The "Go-To" once youthful couple, MG and Liz Bass, has aged today before his eyes into a middle aged married couple. They were visiting his office because they needed answers. What could he tell them to make it all better? Dr. Jefferson sat down at his desk as he prepared to utter the unfortunate message.

Their son, River, arrives at the office to show support for his mother Liz. However, upon hearing the diagnosis as he approached Uncle Jefferson's office, NINE WORDS made him freeze as he was turning the crystal knob. Outside the door, he remained quiet and unseen as the diagnosis clashed cymbals, of despair,

"Liz, I am so sorry…you have Parkinson's disease.

What do you mean Parkinson's disease? You're referring to the old people disease. How did this happen? What caused it? Her mind took off running an "Endless Million Thoughts" marathon with a "no win" finish line. M.G. said, "Leumas, no offense I would really like a second opinion."

He quickly agreed and began processing her paperwork for her to visit the Medical College for further observation. He explained how the neurology specialty team would examine her with a battery of tests. In the meantime, he wanted to prescribe something for her.

Liz quickly refused his prescription and said, prescribe something for what? I need a few more days to process this information. Furthermore, let's make sure we know what is being treated. MG, I feel drained, please take me home.

River quickly leaves the office, hops into his company van with scattered energy drinks on the floor and heads back to work. What a lunch hour. He is devastated. Thoughts are racing through his mind. Jesus, my mother is sick and I've got to help her. How?

MG takes her hand and empathizes, Liz, it will be alright. Remember, with a diagnosis, "The First Cut is the Deepest". However, we look forward to a prognosis of healing.

It's been a long day and you need some rest. Let's go home. Goodnight Lemumas. The three of them embrace as their brother's soft spoken voice, replied, "good night" family." He retreats to his study and finds LaCara sobbing on her chaise lounge he installed for their date night "mystery woman" office visits. He opened a bottle of $600 Cognac and pours two drinks over the rocks. Let's toast to MG and Liz's recovery. God help them and help me understand how you can bring them through this situation! He gulps the drink down holds her close as he throws the glass against the wall, yelling, where is the gift in this God? His wife's tears mix with his mint cologne she loves. She refuses the drink and goes to the window. She sings, His Eye is on the sparrow.

…. the same cologne her sister hates will remind her of her dreadful office visit on the long silent drive home with her head-on MG's shoulder. She turns on the car radio and Linda Ronstadt, famous singer and Parkinson's survivor, song "The First Cut is the Deepest" plays.

STOP! To Work on WJF: Worksheet, Journal and FOCUS at the end of each chapter or CONTINUE.
WJF - Worksheet, Journal & Focus
Manifestation end of Chapter Two:
WJF - Diagnosis versus Prognosis

PRAYER: Pray for 26 seconds on Topic of Focus - Biblical Manifestation: Diagnosis VS. PROGNOSIS

DEVOTION: Take 26 minutes to read Ezekiel 36:25-27. D – DIAGNOSIS

Question: Since a medical doctor can give me a DIAGNOSIS, can he/she give me an accurate PROGNOSIS?

Answer: Your doctor gives you a diagnosis and even attempts an accurate Prognosis. However, only God and our faith can determine an accurate prognosis. See scripture example BELOW.

SCRIPTURE DIAGNOSIS: A New Heart and Spirit - 25"Then I will sprinkle clean water on you, and you will be clean; I will cleanse you from all your filthiness and from all your idols.

SCRIPTURE PROGNOSIS:26"Moreover, I will give you a new heart and put a new spirit within you; and I will remove the heart of stone from your flesh and give you a heart of flesh. 27"I will put My Spirit within you and cause you to walk in My STATUTES and you will be careful to observe my ordinances. Ezekiel 36:25-27

JOURNALIZE AND POLISH YOUR PURPOSE: Explain an illness from your past. What were the diagnosis and the prognosis?

<u>Fish Hook Quote</u>: Why lean on a <u>doctor</u> to give <u>you</u> an accurate <u>Diagnosis</u> and <u>Prognosis</u>, when God made all four?
T. Cobb- Morgan

3

BACK DOWN MEMORY LANE
WJF – Character

Liz IS SITTING on the sofa looking at the family photo album. After arriving home, Liz thought about her diagnosis and her family. They have two grown sons, Carlos and River, and four grandchildren living in the local area.

However, MG also has a strained relationship with a grown daughter, Teal Ivy, who has a husband and two sons. MG has never met Teal Ivy's husband or her children. They reside in Washington, D.C. with her mother Daisy, his ex-wife of Five years before they decided to end in divorce. The only Precious assets they split were Carlos and Teal Ivy

"My life is a mess. I wonder if MG still loves me. Is he still attracted to me? Does he resent the day he met me and came to my house with two new suits for the church yard sale? I recall that day so vividly" …

LIZ at CHILDHOOD HOME – MORNING 1970's
MG, it's a beautiful Saturday morning to make some grass cutting or car washing money, said his best friend Tommy. I need to swing by my

uncle's house to drop off some items for a church yard sale. I would like for you to meet my Uncle Lil Jack.

Sure, remarked a reluctant MG. Once a worldly New Yorker, he found his character challenged to be content and settle down at home as a single father with Carlos and work on his reading. His teacher advised state testing would begin next month for her class.

MG sighed, a struggling Staff Sergeant in the Air Force, he needed to make extra money. He slowly called his babysitter. Besides, Carlos needed new school clothes and he owed Mary, the administrative assistant, Lunch for a special favor.

Since they were cutting grass for other people in the community, he decided to go along for extra money. They knocked on the door.

"Just a minute" Liz yelled as she cut off the vacuum cleaner. In her sexy, raspy southern drawl, Liz said, "Hi yawl come on in Cousin Tommy!

"Hey Liz, how are you?! This is my buddy MG. MG managed to get a stuttered "Hi "out. Hi MG, would you care for some iced tea with lemon? Tommy cut across before MG could respond, "Sorry, no time Liz. We have a long day ahead of us. See you later Cuz."

MG thought to himself, Wow, what a beautiful woman! Her southern drawl sounded like music as she whirled my name around her tongue. I must figure out a way to get back there…. *tonight!*"

Screeeeeeeeeeeech! Was the sound OF HIS hangers dragging across the metal clothing bar! Smitten and anxious to get back to Liz' house, MG found himself in his closet searching for two beautiful suits he had custom made overseas and ripping off the tags. He had to impress the tight jean wearing flight attendant with a bandanna on her head and a cotton tee.

(Liz teases him to this day), "Wow, MG you didn't even know if I had hair!

HE replied, well, I couldn't think of a prettier alopecia model!

STOP! To Work on WJF: Worksheet, Journal and FOCUS at the end of each chapter or CONTINUE.
<u>**Manifestation End of Chapter Three**</u>
CHARACTER

WJF - Worksheet, Journal & Focus

End of Chapter Three

PRAYER: Pray for 26 seconds on Biblical Manifestation for: CHARACTER

DEVOTION: TAKE 26 minutes to read chapter: 26What then shall we say, brothers? When you come together, everyone has a psalm or a teaching, a revelation, a tongue, or an interpretation. All of these must be done to build up the church. I Corinthians 14:26

Question: I am a bible reading beginner and I'm struggling to understand. However, I love to play cards. What is CHARACTER (Integrity) in the game of cards?

Answer: Character is how many bad jokes "Jokers" jump out of your face (mouth), "ACE" (you) and the "King and Queen" are not in the Courts for your JUDGEMENT to face,
To "Jack" you up for bad joke behavior, lucky for you, there was an out of court judgment waiver.
Why? Because in your "Heart of hearts, your poker face" projects a blind stare AND YOU JUST DON'T CARE,
After all no one is watching and, you're at home playing Solitaire!

JOURNALIZE AND POLISH YOUR PURPOSE: Write down character changes you would like to make, as they relate in the game of cards. Which character do you represent: Joker (Never serious about life quests. Ace (on top of your game), and King (Male dignitary), and Queen (Female dignitary or sequence of numbers 1 (Lowest) – 10 (Highest) on character scale?

Fish Hook Quote: Remember, Ace, Character is what is shone, when you are AT THE CASTLE, home alone.
T. Cobb- Morgan

Grannie Hog Maw

Grannie Hog Maw
She's my girl, "she gets me,"
She is a combination of all the special mothers I have inside you see.
They all push me on and give me an "Atta girl"
Stay brave and contribute good to this world.
They tell me to push ahead keep going, push through!
Because we all "got your back" and God has his eye on you!
And He Will Do Great Things Through You.

4

PARKINSON'S OR PARK IN THE SUN?
WJF – Hope

KEEP ON ASKING GOD FOR WHAT YOU WANT!

"Ask, and it will be given to you; seek, and you will find; knock, and it will be opened to you. [8] for everyone who asks receive, and the one who seeks finds, and to the one who knocks it will be opened." Matthew 7:7-8

THE SCRIPTURE RESONATES in Liz's mind as she looks at MG taking a nap on the other end of the sofa. They are in the bedroom of their two-story 100-year-old southern built home in Virginia which is nestled on a couple of acres. Beyond the trees is a Bass fish lake which flows out to the Atlantic Ocean.

The years have been kind to MG. In his sixties, he still has his salt and pepper hair laid back and a thick, questionably "black" moustache. He remains charming, confident, stubborn and UNAFRAID TO ask THE tough questions. He is an excellent caregiver to ME.

I am dearly holding on to my fifties. A people person, I still enjoy friendly conversation with others, sharing my love of art, craft and creations. Normally, front and center, Parkinson's is slowly pushing me back behind the scenes.

I am writing a Romance Comedy screenplay and book for a movie.

The screenplay features my younger son, RIVER. He is attached to four women in "his EAR" (HIS life): His Mother, His Ex, Delilah pushed out by an animated character, his bossy Grannie Hog Maw (MG's mother), his newly found fiancée Eileen and he befriends an animated bass fish named Pink Lady Sassy Bass (His spiritual advisor). Despite their differences, they learn and share life's lessons and experiences during their special friendships.

In the meantime, I am hopeful, persistent and a real-life Parkinson's Survivor. Throughout the story and movie, my whole face IS not revealed. This is indicative of how most disabled individuals hide from the public.

Since My diagnosis, I've learned most my family and friends are challenged with an illness, injury or disease of some type. Those physical WINDS heavily blow at us but they can't knock us down.

MY Husband, Sons, grandchildren, MY crazy funny sisters, hilarious Grannie Hog Ma (MY mother in law), friends and family keep a mental "BASS WIND DEFLECTOR" which diverts the winds and breezes in empathy and humor to encourage each other.

I feel that now my life mission is my voice of advocacy to encourage others, bring awareness to their unique situations and to ask God "Why"? They will begin to manage their struggles that don't happen to us but for us. In our own time, we become empowered survivors by dealing with the challenges of life and their purpose in a positive light OF LOVE, FAITH AND HOPE.

Liz's voiceover speaks, but she is restless, tosses and turns.

Liz pulls down her eye mask and peers over it to see the clock. Her white face cream has dried all over her face and she is wearing a hair bonnet. She zooms in at the television clock. The neon numbers reflect 4:00 a.m. Oh no, I must pee again. It's such a long trip to the bathroom and its only 4:00 a.m.! (She looks over at her husband, MG, snoring and deeply asleep. She puts one foot on the floor and lifts the other. Hunched over, she slowly shuffles over to the bathroom and back to bed.

LIZ is dreaming (Her voice over continues.) Dazed, if I run through this chain of events maybe it will make SENSE...confused, she babbles.

Again, the first five years I ignored my Parkinson's diagnosis (no medications, no special foods and very little stretching or exercise. I was a fool! One day, on my way to work, I pulled over at the mouth of the Hampton Roads Bridge Tunnel. What was I doing there? My mind was as foggy as the weather that day. Feeling uneasy, I called MG. MY hand shook nervously, but I didn't feel nervous.

I CALLED my boss to advise him I was taking a sick day and His voice STILL echoes in her mind.

"Take care of yourself Liz."

I drove straight to the emergency room and MG met me there. That was my last day at work. It's been ten years now and I still hear "take care of yourself Liz."

No matter how much I try to retreat from this, my fifty something year-old body duels with the ravages of this disease. I have stooped posture, a shuffling gait, a stoic look and a right-side tremor. I avoid most social functions unless the event is at home.

My husband has taken on extra roles as "The CCC" caregiver, cook and chauffeur. I never regarded the word soulmate as "gospel" aka "the truth", until now. The words "Soul Mate" should be coined "Toll Mate" by the way life takes its toll on the coins of illness, injury and disease which are spent daily. "In sickness and in health" vows are tested to the edge of your matrimonial cliff. We pray for each other every day.

One day I asked God why He allowed Parkinson's to happen to me. I felt HIM say, Liz, it didn't happen to you, it happened for you. What do you mean God? I need to understand why Parkinson's? Wait! Park-in-Sons! If I can make sense of this and break it down;

1) "Park" means to store, service or leave a vehicle for an appointed time.
2) "In" means inclusion within a space, place or limits.
3) "Son/Sun" means the sun in the sky, an illumination of your idea and plan for me!

Yes, I am the truth and the light. But I'm showing you the Son/Sun in a different form.

Please forgive me Lord, of course you are referring to your Son, Jesus.

Liz, I was referring to your sons. Huh, you mean Carlos and River, God?

I have provided for your grandsons too.

I responded, Really God, REALLY? Oh thank-you God! Now, what am I supposed to do?

You asked me to help you leave a legacy for them. Liz, in return I want you to prepare a message of my love, healing and faith to the world. let me be clear, I need you to encourage and compel the world to love, hope and have faith. I have an overabundance of them stored up in heaven because my children on earth don't realize the keys to their self-empowerment. Just like any budget with surplus, if you don't use it you will lose it! The amazing thing about love, hope and faith is if they would just add prayer, it works! Anything, they ask in my name! "that, is amazing", says an astonished Liz. She immediately engages her assignment without asking God for her healing. Thus, He rewards her faith and patience. He further explains, the key is your gift and passion for the arts – writing, song and art. Remember, with that big imagination I gave you, I have already empowered you with the Gift of storytelling. Learn from me because I did it best with the parables. The world loves a good story to teach, soothe, provoke and leave them dramatized beyond imagination! In fact, you came close when I said "you can't ask, think nor <u>imagine</u> the treasures I have stored up for you. Tell me Liz; are you too afraid to ask for anything else? I thought about getting out of the Wheelchair I have been in for two years.

Oh, of Course. By the way, you will live your dream and you will "walk" again.

The dictionary resurrect means to restore (a dead person) back to life:

GOD KEPT HIS PROMISE. WHEN HIS SON AROSE EASTER WEEKEND MARCH, 2016…so did I!

STOP! To Work on WJF: Worksheet, Journal and FOCUS at the end of each chapter or CONTINUE.

<u>Manifestation End of Chapter Four</u>
WJF - Worksheet, Journal & Focus
Hope

<u>PRAYER</u>: Pray for 26 seconds on Topic of Focus - Biblical Manifestation: HOPE

<u>DEVOTION</u>: TAKE 26 minutes to read chapter and challenge question.

H – HOPE[24] for in this hope we were saved. But hope that is seen is no hope at all. Who hopes for what they already have? [25] But if we hope for what we do not yet have, we wait for it patiently.
[26] In the same way, the Spirit helps us in our weakness. We do not know what we ought to pray for, but the Spirit himself intercedes for us through wordless groans. Romans 8:24-26

Challenge Question One: What message of HOPE did God promise Liz she would do AGAIN?

Challenge Question TWO: Write down a dictionary meaning of HOPE.

Challenge Question THREE: What is the biblical meaning of HOPE?

JOURNALIZE: Write about the message of HOPE you will BELIEVE God for during this 26 Day trial.
My Message OF HOPE is:

Fish Hook Quote:

Hope, then YOU LIVE. LIVE, THEN YOU HOPE.
AS an answer to your dreams, it will be yes, wait or NOPE.
TIME IS NOT ON OUR SIDE,
BUT WE HAD YESTERDAY.
THANK YOU FOR MY FAITH-BASED RIDE
CAUSE TOMORROW COULD BE TODAY.

T. COBB-MORGAN

Vision Board

5

I WILL LIVE MY DREAM
WJF - Faith

I WILL LIVE my dream. I will live my dream! I will live my dream! Liz is in bed.

MG says, Liz, wake up! Are you alright? What is it? Are you stressing your movie screenplay plans again? What is the status of the movie screenplay?

It's going fine dear, replies a shaken Liz. But I fell asleep while writing. I'm still working on the introduction. Please listen to see if I'm on point.

Sure, no problem, a concerned MG.

Liz continues, "I felt a spiritual presence as the splendid sunburst kissed me good morning. The majestic maple tree branches bent down to hug me as the sweet gardenias dew dropped velvety vanilla petals around my feet. Just as I thought this morning could not have been more perfect, God sent a crimson red cardinal bird to serenade my pain away with another gift, this day of healing." (She pauses) OH, MG, no matter how I dress it up there is nothing beautiful about illness, injury or disease!

Babe, that was beautiful. You truly have a gift of bringing words to life. As you have reminded me, the *beauty* begins after the diagnosis and you must convey that to others.

Thank you. But sometimes I still feel so inadequate. What if I missed His calling on my life in pursuing this movie and the soundtracks? I've been thanking HIM three years for my leg healing.

MG looks over his spectacles, Listen, you keep going Liz. God will do the rest. You know there are millions of people suffering who don't know the will of God during their suffering. Sadly, most only feel guilt, shame and escape. They don't know the key to open the door of their purpose. He sends us reminders all the time, this time He chose you. He chose me to take care of you. Let's begin with breakfast. I have turkey bacon, a sunny side up egg, orange marmalade English muffin and berry herbal tea to lift your spirits and ease the stress involved with your book and screenplay.

Oh, honey how thoughtful and what a treat, blushed Liz!

That reminds me, (holds the palm of his hand to his forehead) Honey, I forgot the honey!

Never mind this meal is fit for a queen...I should be able to sweeten it with my finger.

Oh, should I go and find the honey before you burn your finger or (mimics an English accent) sit patiently to witness an act of royalty, my lady? (Teasingly he circles his hands and bows before her).

Liz returns an English accent, SIT my lord and be amazed!

GRANNIE HOG MA Walks in without knocking and says," Yeah, and if I had a Taser gun...you'd both be tased!"

Liz says, "Grannie Hog Ma?" Grannie hog mA puts her hands on her hips and REPLIES, "that's my name, don't wear it out!

Mother, what are you doing here?

Son, Snort, Snort…What the smell? I live here… I have a key so I don't need to ring that "highfalutin" doorbell playing the adventures of Wesley Snipes Rhymes!

Mother, that's Westminster Chimes!

MG, Whatever! Anyway, where is River? I have some Gummi Candy Lures for his tackle box.

Mother, where else could he be? Of course, He's gone fishing… again. Did we "mark" HIM WITH the name River? Sometimes I wonder if he is the "Fish Whisperer!"

Oh really, question's Liz. C'mon MG you know Big Mouth Bass don't talk. Or do they?

Snort, Snort what the smell? What are you two talking about? Maybe I can catch my little puddle – all grown up to a big River! (She yells out of the window.) River! Well, I've got to go to the drug store to pick up some blackberry peach snuff.

Mother, you promised to give up that disgusting habit.

She snorts, oh well, Jerome wasn't built from hay!

MG exasperated, YOU mean Rome wasn't built in a day!

Grannie Hog Maw's eyes rolling up to the ceiling, "Whatever, hand me my imported grasshopper can."

Mother, locusts don't come in a can. What can?!

I beg to differ, MG. They do if you get them on Friday before 5:00 p.m. rush hour out of Jug head Johnson's car trunk…but you must use a pair of pliers to get your cans out (She reaches for a can from behind bed headboard and spits in it).

Mother, please stop doing that. Furthermore, stop eating canned food out of car trunks! You can get poisoned by Botulism.

Grannie Hog Ma scoffed at MG and held her snuff filled mouth up and said," MG leaves out good ole' Bob Chiasm? What? What are you saying MG, he wouldn't do that! He is an upstanding Mexican man. He even changed his name from Manwell Hacienda Pedro's to Bob Chism trustworthy, noteworthy and now cash worthy city Council man. If my memory serves me right, didn't he get rid of that bright red leisure suit and bought a trustful brown councilman suit. If he wasn't married to that blonde gold digging queen Sham pain in the neck from the trailer park, I'd champagne him, I mean campaign him!

Nonsense! Mother, stop stereotyping, it's nothing but racism! Does this mean you're changing your name to Sally Bessie Mae Jones? MG quickly realizes her loss of hearing is responsible for the senseless dialogue and changes the subject. Mother, you need a new hearing aid.

Grannie Hog Maw squeals, "No, I don't. I hear what I want to hear."

Immediately, the atmosphere of the room changes from blissful breakfast morning to "Gunfight high Noon at the Bass Corral ranch." Sheriff Liz jumps in waving her white flag for agreement among the two, "MG, she has a point there."

Outlaw Grannie Hog maw is surprised that Liz is defending her and not Deputy MG. Snort, Snort, what the smell? I have a hearing aid and it works just fine. I took it from your daddy.

MG bows his head and comments, "my poor father, God rest his soul" as draws an imaginary cross over his body.

Snort! Snort! What the smell? She replies and sings, "Papa was a rolling stone" your daddy ain't dead. He ran off with the neighbor's wife and my diamond chip RING! And by the way you ain't Catholic" either. You're Take me to the Water Baptist!

A confused MG questions, "He did?" (Pause) I'm not? Mother, this ridiculous story is a farce. I went to Catholic school, attended my Daddy's funeral and I don't recall you having any diamonds.

MG, first your school was a shot house but Ms. Mary's daughter babysat you while studying first semester World Religion. The funeral was for your Daddy's brother, Uncle James aka Jimmy Beam Bass. And, for the record I don't fart, I poot…BAAAWRANK or booty burp!

BAAABOOM! There, now that's settled. I would have a diamond if my son would buy me a mother's ring with my birthstone, a diamond!

Liz exclaims, Grannie Hog Ma, you were born in October. Your birthstone is Pink Zircon!

Meanwhile, Poor MG, still in mild shock raises an epiphany, "So that's why Lil MARY TOLD me the Pope is now Bishop of Detroit. Is my daddy my Uncle Jimmy Bean Hog Head Cheese? Mama, you still have bad gas! By the way we will pick up your ring tomorrow. Liz and I will buy one for you as hers.

MG, you know I love Liz so don't take this the wrong way. Men marry women who remind them of their mothers. You obviously married Liz for that reason and the BPB (Brown Paper Bag) Test. (She pulls out a brown plastic bag). "Imagine this over Liz's face, oops Snort! Snort! What the smell? I mean beside Liz face. She isn't lighter so she's not a redbone (attracts dark men) and she's not darker than this bag so she's not an African Treat (attracts redbone and white men). Throw in her bubbly personality, that "Rise and Shine" southern drawl song she sings before noon, ugh! And that perfect smile she trumps both sides, MG, watch her!

Liz yells, "I can hear you Grannie Hog Maw!"

GRANNIE HOG MA yells, "I'm out …Deuces! I need to catch a flight on the next thing smoking! Judging by my tastes, my tall, rich, creamy colored Boo is out there, somewhere, looking for me … in Scandinavia!" MG remarks, did we learn anything from Dr. Martin Luther King? It's not the color of our SKIN; it's the content of our character! What about honesty, integrity and helping others?

Well son, I am quite a character, honest enough to tell you with integrity that I will help you find my diamond mother's ring! I'm out. Oh, Liz, I enjoyed the story you are writing about your ancestry you shared with River. Good story. She Yells, OUT the window, RIVER!!

Poem/Song: I AM A SHULAMITE

What a beautiful black girl.
Or, she is so pretty, but dark.
We can kick it in a movie or maybe in park
Who is your friend? … Hey light skin – red bone in the house
Somebody please tell me what's this inner racism all about.

Do we need to go back to Jesus Loves the little children of the world?
Red, Brown, yellow, black and white, all so precious in His sight,
Jesus Loves you little boy and little girl.

I like to introduce you to the darkest most beautiful woman in the world,
King Solomon was struck by her beauty, had to make her his wife, this gorgeous girl.

I am a Shulamite; I am dark and lovely,
King Solomon loves me with all his might, but there were no sparks from me.
There is a lesson we all learn in time, speak to me daughters of the divine, do not awaken love,
God said all virtue is mine.

I am an African American, brought here against my will.
Men all over the world love me so.
And some of them do still.
Strength, wisdom and royalty I befriend,
I'm more than hair, lips and skin?
Do not awaken love; God said all virtue is mine.

I Am Latin American, cheated out of my property,
For guns, whiskey and grass
Our Chief stripped of dignity and class.
There is a lesson we all learn in time,
Speak to me to others of the divine
Do not awaken love; God said all virtue is mine.

I am the black sheep of the family, but nobody looks like me,
and I look like nobody.
God says you're beautifully and wonderfully made,
Listen to me Children I make no mistakes.
There is a lesson we all learn in time,
All will bow down to, The Divine.

STOP! To Work on WJF: Worksheet, Journal and FOCUS at the end of each chapter or CONTINUE.

WJF - Worksheet, Journal & Focus
WJF - Faith
<u>**Manifestation End of Chapter 5**</u>
"I WILL LIVE MY DREAM!

Prayer: Pray for 26 seconds on Topic of Focus – Biblical Manifestation: FAITH (See "Fin ABC KEY.)

DEVOTION: For as the body without the spirit is dead, so is faith without works is dead also James 2:26

SCRIPTURE:
11 Now faith is the substance of things hoped for, the evidence of things not seen. Hebrews 11:1

Challenge Question One: What does it mean to have the faith of a mustard seed? (See Matthew 17:20.)
20"Because you have so little faith." He answered.
"For truly I tell you, if you have faith the size of a mustard seed, you can say to this mountain, 'Move from here to there,' and it will move. Nothing will be impossible for you." Matthew 17:20…

Challenge Question TWO: What do you believe is your measure of faith?

Challenge Question THREE: Read the following definition of FAITH found in Dictionary.com:
This is belief not based on proof. Belief in God or in the doctrines or teachings of religion.

JOURNALIZE: Write about an Act of Faith you witnessed.

Fish Hook Quote: Faith is your body as it takes that colossal leap (Works) and your heart through the spirit whispers "YES" out loud, but your head and soul yells "examine me" before the crowd!
T. COBB MORGAN

Riddle:
Q: Why are Big Mouth Bass So Smart?
A: Because They Swim in Schools!

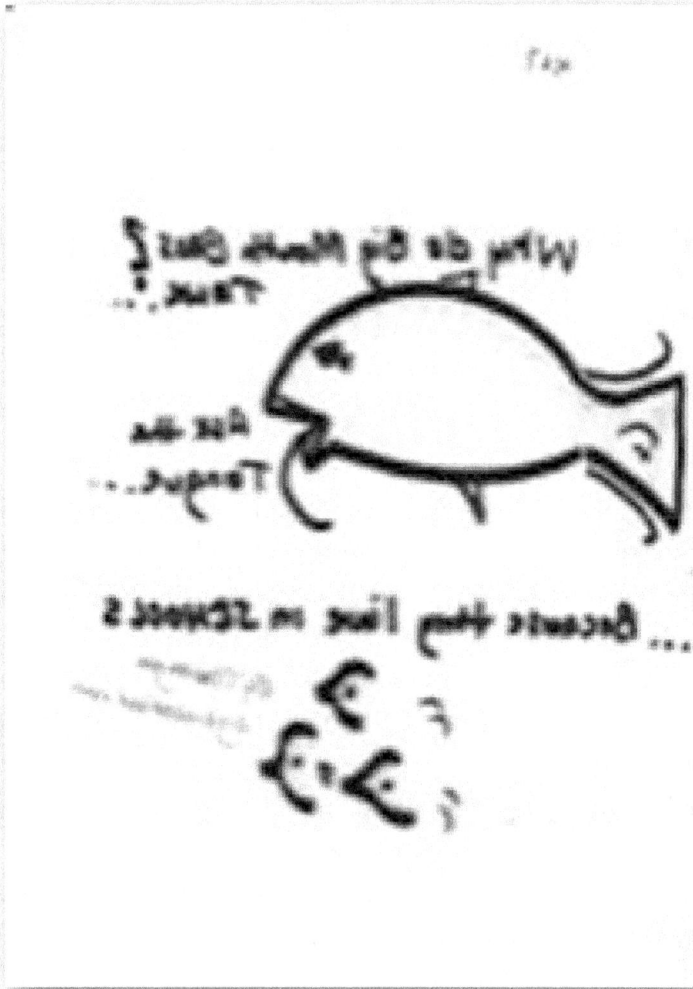

6

I Thank God Big Mouth Bass Don't Talk, or Do They?
WJF - Tongue

River is walking through the woods and the progression of his life evolves as a child, as a teen-ager and as a young adult. The scene opens with the song, "I Thank God That Big Mouth BASS Don't TALK, OR DO THEY?" It shows park like setting with lush trees and greenery. A dirt path leads to an embankment which features a small pier on the river. Pond (Inner Child I), Lake (Inner Child II) and River walk toward the pier in three parts. The walk demonstrates how many years he has grown up walking to the pier beginning at age eight, age Seventeen and now age Twenty-nine.

All three, Pond, Lake and River, are sporting the same look wearing a white tank top shirt, relaxed loose jeans, brown belt, desert boots and their "lucky khaki fishing hat" with bass fishing pins and fish lures around the brim and a hanging chin strap from ear to ear. As they trek to the River, all three have a stern face AND TUNNEL vision gaze stare. River has his PBJ sandwich and energy drink cooler in one hand and a fishing pole in the other.

A 1/3rd through the PARK. The Pond, Inner Child I: The 8 yr. Old character is a cute kid He is wise beyond his years and the older people say, "he has been here before". He is intelligent, perceptive and somewhat shy at times. He is learning core old school values. He is shown as his 8-yr. old child self, initiating 1/3 the walk to the river with his Rottweiler puppy, "Bear". Pond sharply turns and appears as Lake a 17-yr. old, (Inner Child II) CONTINUING the walk through the woods.

Wow, said Pond, what a wonderful story Mom told me. Our ancestry derived from a royal tribe, the TerLyndosos in Africa. Her "many greats" grandmother came to Jamestown in the 1600's. Her father, King TerLyndoso was promised that his young 15-yr old daughter would have a better life, education and medical care for her "Shaking Palsy" in America. She kissed her mother and father goodbye. They gave her a birthday dowry of 15 gold coins encrusted with diamonds to pay for her services in America. It was a tiny ivory box encased in animal skin and bordered with animal teeth a symbol of "sheer grit and grind courage." As the ship came ashore she jumped to the ground and ...

(Lake jumps down from hill on his path), the 17 yr. old CHARACTERS, is a good-looking young man. He is smart; athletic, has quick wit complete with a million-dollar smile. He is growing up fast recognizing the girls. He recognizes core old school values and does his best to ignore them. He is walking to the river with his mid-size Rottweiler dog, "Bear.")

Lake rises and imagines the young princess as she looks up and around at her new home, America. She immediately caught the attention of a ship master's son's blue eyes. He raced over to her and spoke but her English was limited. They became close friends and she could stay in the mansion. Princess TerLyndoso was given a Christian NAME, Sarah Belle and her last name was the plantation name Morgan. She and Luke, a physician, were secretly married and had a son, Kristopher TerLynDoso Morgan. Since interracial marriage was forbidden Luke also "formally" married Sarah Belle's best friend, Lily White, the arrangement worked out well until she became pregnant, but not by her "husband" Luke. She was seeing Luke's best friend and ship assistant, Samuel Black. Since Samuel's Blackness reached far beyond his last name, their relationship was forbidden as well except for "breeding". In the middle of the night, they fled to Canada.

RIVER, 26 yr. old, finishes the walk. The character (River III) is handsome, tall 6'3", muscular and has a gorgeous smile – a cool laid back bad boy type but practices core old school values. He is funny and a tad bit immature at times. The camera starts at his boots and proceeds up toward his face. (Music stops to song: "I Thank God that Big Mouth Bass Don't Talk. Written by T. Cobb Morgan) As Lake approaches 2/3rd through the walk he appears as his 26-yr. old adult self and full-size Rottweiler, "Bear."

The family always said Grandma Sarah loved to fish on Sarah's Nile which is really the James River, King Terlyndoso's English name. I feel her presence on the James River. Old folklore suggests she fell into the river and her dress got caught up in an old fishing net wire. Fearful of drowning she got out her dress and swam to shore. The wire caused a great loss of blood and she died. Supposedly the coins are still there. Normally, I would be snorkeling in the James River exploring for "treasure", but I need to ease my mind regarding the diagnosis of my mother's illness. I'm going fishing today.

Song: I Thank God, That Big Mouth Bass Don't Talk,
Or DO They?
Written By: T. Cobb Morgan
LizLL03@aol.com

I'm going fishing today, down by the river (Good God! Lawd),
This is my therapy, to have coffee with God, and catch come
bass and cod.
Got my pole and my gummi lures and my boat the Sarah Belle,
Confession's good for the soul, to clear some lies I had to TELL!

I thank God, that fish don't judge and they can't hear,
The rumbling pain inside I feel.
A fish has never held me to my walk,
I thank God that big mouth bass don't talk...or do they?

I'm going fishing today, down by the river (Good God! Lawd),
This is my therapy, to have coffee with God, and catch come
bass and cod.
Got my pole, my gummi lures and my boat the Sarah Belle,
Confessions good for the soul, to clear some lays I had to tell!
I thank God, that fish don't judge and they can't hear,
The rumbling pain inside I feel.
A fish has never held me to my walk,
Song: Page 2of2 Written by T. Cobb Morgan
I thank God that big mouth bass don't talk...or do they?
Girl, you got me pondering for so long,
Trying to figure out just what went so wrong?
Love has drained my heart... it's a shame for today,
My sad story is the prize catch. You girl got away!

This is my therapy, to have coffee with God, and catch come bass and cod.
Got my pole and my gummi lures and my boat the Sarah Belle,
Confessions good for the soul, to clear some lies I had to TELL!

I thank God, that fish don't judge and they can't hear,
The rumbling pain inside I feel.
A fish has never held me to my walk,
I thank God that big mouth bass don't talk. (End of song.)

River approaches the pier, places his cooler down and positions his pole.

Man, what a nice day for fishing, remarks River. I can smell the bass. It's pre-spawn, early morning and just cloudy enough to shelter the bass to come out to feed and nest. My fishing pole line is in position and is tugging already! If this continues the bass will have to wait their turn and start taking numbers. It's all good, come to me, baby. I got you and plenty of gummi candy lures!

The fish are biting right on time; one is really pulling the line. River must reel the line just right to get this fish in, a feisty one. (talks to himself) hold the line steady river, tug, and reel her in.

Gotcha! Now let me release this hook...steady girl. (He holds her in his hand. He opens his hand she perches in his palm.)

(The fish on Rivers' line is "Pink Lady" and is an animated sassy PINK BASS fish. sings and dances. She has a noticeably disabled extra fin that sticks up like an antenna. She starts Dancing while perched in River's hand).

Finally! Wow, aren't you gorgeous...and PINK! I've never seen such a pink bass before. (RIVER STARES AT HER) your scales are hues of light iridescent pink to dark rose. You have a blonde ponytail twist; large eyes are adorned with long sweeping lashes and you have the biggest mouth I've ever seen on a bass. I'm going to call you Pink Lady Sassy Bass, with your big mouthed thick self! (He whips out his cell phone) I've got to get a selfie of this! Do you bass fish realize how many secrets, stories, songs and selfies I've shared with you? I thank God that big mouth bass don't talk! Or do they?

You tell me. By the way, who are you calling a thick big mouth, sasses Pink Lady Sassy BASS?

River is startled looks around as Pink Lady perches in the palm of his hand.

A shocked River replies, you can talk! Am I hearing things? No, I heard you talk!

Sarcastically, good catch and good observation. Of course, I talk! Did you think I'd have this much mouth and not talk? Besides I could not hold it in any longer and bear that long drawn-out sonnet of yours. What in the name of King Neptune's River is a selfie?

River slowly responds in disbelief, it's a picture you take of yourself and/ or include others in your photograph.

The fish confused, why? What a waste! Just come down to the RIVER AND look at your reflection in the water all day! Duh! Now listen River, you can't share my talking secret with anyone. Besides, I wouldn't utter a word in the presence of other humans. I will only glob fish Latin glob, GLUB" if you bring others to the pier. I'll speak only to you for purpose of doing well!

How did you know my name Pink Lady? Why do you trust me? And, while we are being honest why do you have an extra undeveloped fin?

River, you have been coming to this spot on the river as your place of solace since you were a little boy. I've lived in this river for quite a few years. I've heard your name whispered, blessed, yelled, screamed and cursed more times than I care to admit!

River says really?

Who wouldn't trust a grown man who uses gummi candy lures for bait and gingerly places the female bass back in the water to carry on the circle of life. The female bass celebrates you River! …by the way, when are you getting rid of that dumb hat?!

Sorry, the lucky hat stays…a gift from my tour in Afghanistan, defends River. It kept me cool in the desert and hopeful to make it back to fish again in Virginia. So, you like the gummi lures, huh?

Nice touch, chuckles Pink Lady especially during our special lady bass times. You seem to understand when our gills are swollen, our fins hurt and we occasionally get a sweet tooth for your gummi lures when the sweet vine grass is low in the river. Now as for my disability concerning my fin it keeps me humble. Growing up I was bullied and teased in the school of fish. Kid fish can be so cruel. Eventually, I decided to laugh with the other fish and guess what?

What? says River with interest.

Pink Lady quickly reacts, they stopped teasing me! What a relief. I quickly joined their school of fish. It was awful and pretentious. I'm not a follower, I'm a leader and so are you River! I seek out other fish and mentor them to take pride in themselves and to manage their disability. I consider myself a disabled fin survivor. The key is to take care of yourself and live your life to the fullest! River can you keep a secret?

Sure, promises River.

Okay, hold your finger to my fin and say I declare…

River buys in as he verifies her intentions, wait a minute, don't you mean "I swear?"

Pink Lady snaps, didn't your Mother teach you not to swear? Now pay attention and listen River! Work with me! I'll hold my fin to your finger. Now brace yourself River and wait for the magical jolt. Watch the sparkles fill the air! Look, the sparkles are bursting into colorful rays of the rainbow. Red Watermelon, Juicy Orange, Banana Yellow, Green Apple, Blue Berry, Indigo Grapes and Plum Violet!

Wow, Pink Lady. That was awesome! Where did you get those Fireworks? Don't just stand THERE; let me have a few of your fireworks for later. What kind are they? Was the smoke coming from the cherry smokers? Your Fire Rockets had to be the grand finale of the rainbow colors?

River, do you *see* any fireworks? That was our fin to fist bump friendship magic. River, MY FRIEND THAT is the power of a fin bump. As you would say a fist Pump! (Song: The Power of Fist bump plays. -BY T. COBB Morgan)

SONG: THE POWER OF A FIST BUMP!
Written by T. Cobb Morgan - LizLL03@aol.com

I never understood the power of a fist bump. A fist bump? Yes, a fist bumps!

People never seem to scowl at a fist bump…at a fist bump…baby.

(Chorus continues, we go around and around with a fist bump, yes, a fist bumps! Stopping to greet whomever we see. Tell me what in the world is a fist bump? Yes, a fist bumps. Glad, you took the time to humor Me.!)

A strange phenomenon has entered he land, called a fist bump. What in the world is a fist bump? Let's just ask Grannie HOG MAW. We must find out what it is today. Excuse me mam what is a fist bump?

Well, a fist bump is something like a handshake, and your knuckles ache. Oh, and your skin might break. Oh, look at the time for goodness sakes. Bye, bye Sunny.

Sunny? BREAKING NEWS!

I've never understood the power of a fist bump. A fist bump? Yes, a fist bump!

People never seem to scowl at a fist bump…at a fist bump…baby.

Handshakes give goodwill to business, but a fist bump clears up resistance.

E meaning of a friendship was given to River and Pink LADY RELEASING the magic of healing SUNBURSTS SO cool was even a little crazy!

I never understood the power of a fist bump. A fist bump? Yes, a fist bump! By T. Cobb Morgan Lizll03aol.com

A dazed RIVER turns to Pink Lady that was magical, enchanting and bewitching! Cool.

Pink Lady confides, my mother told me that my disabled fin possesses magical powers! But I must only use it to do good in an emergency. In the meantime, I use it to gather gravel and tiny shells to make bling fish jewelry.

You're into "bling" Pink Lady?

Ye ah, look at ME; it has made me quite u*nique in Coral Reef village manor.* We have so much fun! We get together on weekends and eat, laugh and dance! You must stop by sometime for a bowl of my gumbo.

River answers, ANYTIME. In fact, my dad makes a spicy gumbo.

Pink Lady boasts, well mine is famous for Frog, Insect and Sea Grass. We must celebrate our new friendship! We can karaoke "Shootie and the Blowfish," play "Go Fish cards" or listen to the symbol "King" formerly known as King Neptune. I believe you have the artist formerly known as "Prince."

I'd love to celebrate our friendship Pink Lady. That would be Awesome.

You see River, you and people in general; place too much emphasis on being perfect and thin. Just saying, most fish like to keep it real. You don't see Sock Eyed Salmon getting lid surgery, Puffer fish getting liposuction or Swordfish getting a nose job! (Emphatic) Do you? Do you?!

Uh, no, says River.

Pink Lady advises, well then, there you go! Speaking of go, I've got to get swimming River. I have an appointment to get my gills massaged and my mouth widened. Maybe even a shot of collagen.

River catches her words, but I thought you said you and other fish like to keep it real? (He is cut off by Pink Lady)

River, pay attention, I said MOST fish. However, a girl bass like me tends to be a little higher maintenance! It takes a lot to be me! But don't tell my secret. The village fish think I naturally look like this!

River throws his hands in the air and surrenders, Women!

What did you say River?

Uh, ER, frantic for words, River stammers, that I would love to have a fresh lemon. Also, your secret is safe with me Pink Lady, I wouldn't dare have a hand, nor shall I say a fin in letting your fans down. (Playful flirting) You're a bad fish Pink LADY!

River, don't even think about it…besides you couldn't afford me… (Sings and dances away. She jumps into the water and her head is exposed.) See you around River! Oh, the answer to your question is 1,527 (She starts swimming away).

River puzzled, what question?

She winks your secrets, stories, songs and selfies!

RIVER SMILES see you tomorrow Pink Lady!

Pond, Rivers seven-year-old Inner Child, amazed with the entire dialogue, says "Cool. Did you hear that fish talk"?

(Lake is 17-year-old Inner Child Voice Over which is assumed throughout script) Lake pulls off his earbuds while listening to music.

Dude, we just cleared the pink elephant from his head. Now, is there a pink fish?

(River and his inner children exit to get in his company van and drive off.)

FADE OUT

STOP! To Work on WJF: Worksheet, Journal and FOCUS at the end of each chapter or CONTINUE.
Manifestation of the End of Chapter Six

I Thank God Big Mouth Bass Don't Talk, or Do They?
WJF - Tongue

PRAYER: Pray for 26 seconds on Topic of Focus - Biblical Manifestation: Tongue (SEE "" T" – tongue in THE ABC KEY.)

DEVOTION: TAKE 26 minutes to read designated chapter, question or comment.
Proverbs 31:26 she opens her mouth with wisdom; and in her tongue, is the law of kindness. Who IS THIS WOMAN?

JOURNALIZE AND POLISH YOUR PURPOSE: Explain a past situation that you should have held your tongue?

Fish Hook Quote:

The tongue is the only untamed creatures I know that can run many miles and never get tired,
Kill you with venom of words, while pretending to admire,
Will, tell you the truth and still be a liar
And won't offer you spit as it sets you in fire!
BY LizOcean Bass

T. COBB MORGAN

7

You're Gonna Win!
WJF – Just Trust God

FADE IN

EXT. RIVER PIER - AFTERNOON

PINK LADY IS swimming along when she sees the sea alarm lights flashing and hears a Blue Heron alarm warning lights illuminating huge neon DANGER, DANGER flashing! The fish are swimming frantically in all directions. She looks up to see the huge bird shadow over her. He descends upon her and swipes her with his giant claw. She jumps in between two rocks and slides down narrowly escaping his sharp spear-like bill.

Pink Lady, screams, Oh my goodness! It's a Blue Heron bird! Get away from me you bass eating prehistoric Pterodactyl!

She quickly dives between two rocks and hits rock bottom and echoes as she falls.

Help!

The Blue Heron lands upon the rock trying hard to spear between them but his bill is too big. He loses interest and flies away. After one hour Pink Lady manages to pull her body up onto the rock. She is injured but risks it hoping to see River for help.

River? River are you there?! I'm hurt rea lly bad. (She's coughing and her appearance is disheveled, tired and weak).

(Her fin is wounded and she has no strength. She falls in and out of consciousness.)

EXT. RIVER PIER- NIGHT

FADE OUT

SONG: She sings "You're Gonna Win" BY T. Cobb Morgan. Never give up on faith Hope and love.

YOU'RE GONNA WIN – By T. Cobb Morgan
LizLL03@aol.com

Woe is me, the wind has been let out my sail
my fin is caught into a rock,
And I don't think I'm going to prevail.
Woe is me, the wind has been let out my sail
my fin is caught into a rock,
And I don't think I'm going to prevail.
But when life hands you disappointment you will see
My own best friend is me!
Woe, not me, the wind is back in my sail
I'm flying Free and I now see
My own best friend is me!
By T. Cobb Morgan LizLL03@aol.com

STOP! To Work on WJF:. Worksheet, Journal and FOCUS at the end of each chapter or **CONTINUE.**
Chapter Seven: You're Gonna Win

<u>Manifestation End</u>
WJF Just Trust

PRAYER: Pray for 26 seconds on Topic of Focus - Biblical Manifestation: Just Trust God

DEVOTION: Take 26 minutes to read designated chapter, question or comment.
Vindicate ME OH LORD FOR me, O LORD, for I have walked in my integrity, And I have trusted in the LORD without wavering.
2Examine me, O LORD, and try me; Test my mind and my heart. Psalm 26:1-2

<u>JOURNALIZE AND POLISH YOUR PURPOSE</u>: Explain a past situation that you should have trusted God for an answer. How did it turn out? Will you try God the next time?

<u>Fish Hook Quote</u>: Why trust man with your body, spirit and soul, when you can trust the one who made them and a temple for you to behold.
T. COBB MORGAN

PART 2

8

IT'S BEEN A HARD DAY'S NIGHT
WJF – Opportunity Knocks

CHIRP! CHIRP! CHIRP…is the sound of sleeping River's alarm clock going off. He leans over and hits the snooze button. "Too easy sergeant he mumbles. Again, he is having night mares from his Army days in Afghanistan. He has been attending "Inner Child therapy" to deal with mild complications of PTSD, Post-Traumatic Stress disorder. River has not only one inner child, he has two. Pond is his seven-year-old inner child and Lake is his seventeen-year-old inner child.

Alright let's move says Pond shaking River on the shoulder. "Hey buddy wake up! I need my coffee to get my day going. (Holding his nose) Peppy Le Phrew you need a shower!"

A stuffy nose River sits up and salutes, thinking he is in the military back in Iraq. He begins shouting) "Sir, too easy. Yes, Sir we will be dressed in five minutes. No Sir we did not oversleep. Soldiers fall in line!" His morning allergies are acting up again with post drip and an aching stomach.

Lake laughs, Man, you should have filed for a disability sleep apnea, now wake up!

River kicks the cover off, Oh no! I have overslept again. Do I have time for a shower?

Are you freaking kidding me...a shower? Man, you better hit low and let the deodorant flow. Brush your teeth and walk out the DOH!

(River is hurrying about his bedroom putting on clothes, getting coffee and brushing his teeth. Grabs a handful of antacids.)

River shakes his head, Man, where did the weekend go?

River arrives at naval base for work grabs his dock team leader hard hat, cargo suit and clipboard. Team river is already working on pallets to load onto navy ship. Three members of the special challenges group (government grants allocated for mentally and physically challenged individuals to gain work experience and training via inclusion with other teams) are huddled in a corner discussing possible layoffs according to the rumor mill. River sees group and quickly disperses them to assignment groups.

As River approaches the team he smiles, Good morning team, what the heck is going on over here? River gives special consideration to the team even when reprimanding them. These pallets aren't going to load themselves. Let's get back to work. By the way, did you all have a good weekend? Hey, we need to plan a team production party at the bowling alley soon. Pizza and wings WILL BE on my TAB, YEAH, baby!

Special Team Leader Alfred speaks with a lisp while Edith and Mordechai chime in, River you know we can't attend.

Why? inquires River.

River, is it true that we may be laid off because the grant money is running out? What are we going to do?

River answers, Listen, currently there are no layoffs pending. However, if you don't get to work, you will cause your own layoff due to poor performance. Now come on let's get to work!

River walks to Supervisor Mills office to get an update. His boss has an uncanny striking resemblance to Michael J. Fox, Parkinson's survivor.

River's boss is on the phone with someone else but yelling outside his office. Hey, River meet me in my office in five minutes.

Yes sir. (Five minutes' elapses. River knocks on the door frame although the door is open but Supervisor Don Mills is still on the phone with his back to the door and finally hangs up. (River walks in)

River I'll make this quick. Although your team numbers look good our budget cuts in other areas were disappointing to say the least. Our bonuses were nearly cut in half! To make matters worse we need to cut an additional 6% in salaries i.e., The *Special Needs Team.*

RIVER

River in disbelief, what?! C'mon Don. They're depending on these jobs to support their families. We chose these candidates to be independent of government assistance and swim on their own. Now we leave them to tread water with no hope of a rescue raft?

Sorry Bud, rafts don't fit into budget. Listen River, they will either sink or swim. So, if you want to talk about treading water then help me find the scum company of pirates whom are illegally dumping in the BAY! Corporate has been all over me to get to bottom of this. In the meantime, I expect you to make the cut by Thursday. Those individuals will therefore try to scan classified ads on Friday rather than stew in pity the whole weekend. Let's get to work. Don waits for River to leave. He remarks, "Damn my fellow republicans in the congress, they're cutting out all the special programs." What an ugly situation, got my muscles so stiff. Where are my Parkinson drugs? He runs his fingers BACK

THROUGH his hair in frustration. Those poor people are going to lose their jobs and benefits. I can't even afford to quit working because my medical would be cut off for Parkinson's and I'm not ready to sit home on disability yet.

River's phone rings as he approaches him office. Hello? Hi Delilah. What? Slow down so that I can understand you babe. Ok your flight for your modeling session leaves early in the morning. You want me to stop by Eileen's flower shop to pick up silk flower sample bouquets. Okay, but please text the address to my phone. What do you mean I don't sound excited about our wedding plans? Babe really? Look, it's been a long day and I'm exhausted. Let's not argue before your trip. Hello? Delilah? (She hung up on him. River puts his cell phone away and gets antacids out of drawer).

Pond throws up his arms, Women! Lake chimes in, MAN; I hope he has a key to unlock that ball and Chain.

POND AND LAKE (IN UNISON)
He needs two. A regular and a spare!

River looks at back of the chair. Now where did I leave my jacket? He looks in the office closet. Why is it not here? Ah man, I left it at the River bank yesterday while talking to Pink Lady! Maybe I can swing by there and still make it to the flower shop. He heads out the door.

FADE OUT

STOP! To Work on WJF: Worksheet, Journal and FOCUS at the end of each chapter or CONTINUE.

Manifestation end of Chapter Eight
"IT'S BEEN A HARD DAY'S NIGHT"
WJF – Opportunity knocks!

PRAYER: Pray for 26 seconds on Topic of Focus - Biblical Manifestation: Opportunity knocks!

DEVOTION: TAKE 26 minutes to read designated chapter, question or comment.

My Sheep will know my voice John 10:25-28
" 25 Jesus answered them, "I told you, and you do not believe. The works that I do in my Father's name bear witness about me, 26 but you do not believe because you are not among my sheep. 27 My sheep hear my voice, and I know them, and they follow me. 28 I give them eternal life, and they will never perish, and no one will snatch them out of my hand.

JOURNALIZE AND POLISH YOUR PURPOSE: Think and write about a great opportunity you were given and how you reacted.

Fish Hook Quote:

> AN Opportunity is not like a bus,
> It doesn't come every 15 minutes
> THAT'S for sure,
> SO, WHEN OPPORTUNITY KNOCKS HONEY YOU
> BETTER get up and ANSWER THE DOOR!

T. Cobb-Morgan

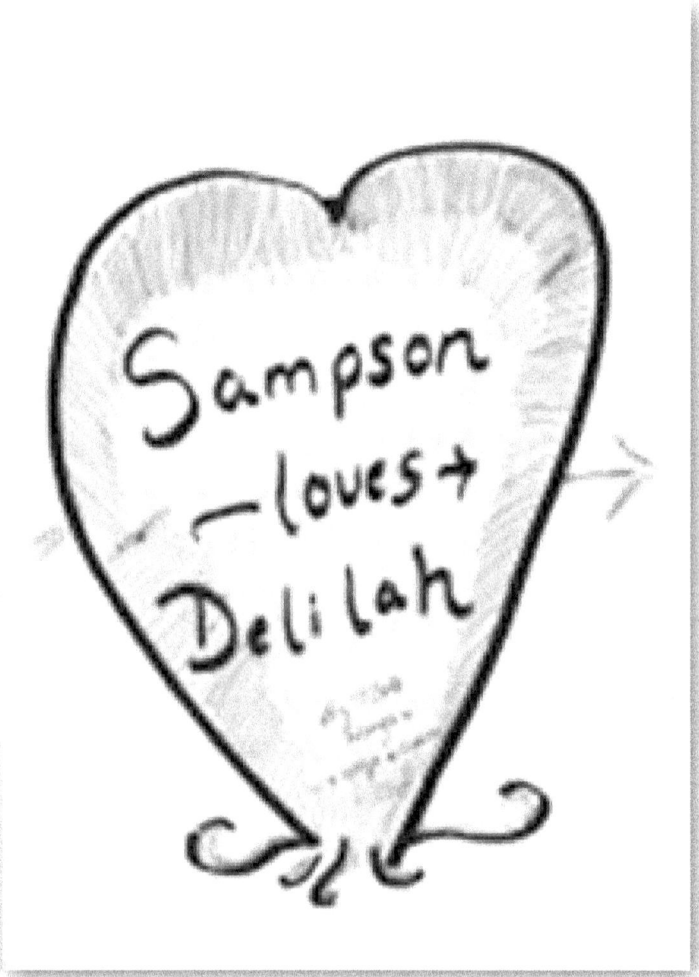

9

WATCH OUT SAMPSON HERE COME'S DELILAH!
WJF – You're In-Sane

DELILAH SAMPSON, RIVER'S fiancée' of five years, has been having a six-month affair with, Larkson Nedo, his best friend since 7th grade.

Delilah is pursuing a modeling career and works part-time at a local bar, she is a self-absorbed, trendy shopaholic and obsessed with her size two frame.

Larkson is a disabled army veteran and current truck driver/contractor. He is a soft-spoken, sly, easily persuasive intellect.

Delilah hangs up the phone on River and is in bed with Larkson. That man infuriates me to no end yells Delilah. Baby, can't I just end this fake engagement with River now over the phone and leave for Miami? I have the perfect little rice designer dress for our perfect justice-of-the-peace elopement. Then I, Mrs. L. A. Nedo, will be shopping for her condo. Our Baby Nedo twins Kim and Kanye will love their new home. I can't wait to flash my two-carat cushion cut diamond engagement ring this evening to those dinner party peasants.

Larkson replies, so much as I would like to, we can't disrespect River like that. We will tell him at dinner as planned. Focus, we must stick to the plan so that he doesn't get suspicious nor second guess our intentions. That will cause him to pull back. Also, speaking of pulling back, we need to pull back on spending. Your most recent ring and the yorkie twin puppies were quite pricey and we need to discuss a budget.

She sits up and begs, Larkson, please stop, you are beginning to sound like River. I hate the word budget. Now, getting to River's "respect", don't you think it's a little too late for River's respect? Where was my respect when he stood me up for senior prom?

Larkson, surprised at her petty ten-year grudge. How many years ago was that?

Delilah continues incessantly, or when he sold the NFL game tickets I gave him for his birthday? Or when he played me for a fool with the D, C. Calendar Triplets, Winter, Spring, Summer…I couldn't believe you'd "Fall" for that, Chuckles Larkson.

Delilah fumes, you think it's funny? Well, who's laughing now? Yeah baby, I got the ultimate revenge of living well! Ha, HA on that!

He responds, listen BABY; let's face it the women will always flock around River. He's the typical tall, dark and handsome prototype candidate. But when it comes to the game, he sucks eggs! His lies don't stick and he's awful at cheating! Why, because he's a hopeless romantic! River is still wandering around the palace with the size six glass slippers in his palm looking for his soulmate princess.

Well, too bad, teases Delilah. He must keep looking for my designer slippers. They don't come in glass.

Larkson, under his breath, says, nor a size six.

She rolls her eyes.

Larkson in a trance babbles on about River. And, it doesn't stop there. Their relationship should "mean" something and their union must make sense! She must be pretty as a sunrise, her ways pure as snow and smell like rain! Poor fella, he will still be looking for that perfect woman and not dating her when our two children are grown.

Della smirks; I hope you mean our yorkies Kim and Kanye because I'm not ruining my figure with two crumb snatching kids! So, what do you think about that Larkson Nebo? (She rubs his back).

He remarks, I think we should be getting ready for dinner tonight. Especially before you write an emotional check you can't void nor cash! He turns and FACES HER and with his body guides her to the wall and they kiss. Besides, we wouldn't want to keep River, the Fish Whisperer, (They chuckle.)

STOP! To Work on WJF: Worksheet, Journal and FOCUS at the end of each chapter or CONTINUE.

Manifestation end of Chapter Nine
<u>"WATCH OUT SAMPSON</u>
<u>HERE COMES DELILAH"</u>
WJF - You're in sane

Prayer: Pray for 26 seconds on Topic of Focus - Biblical Manifestation: You're In Sane **DEVOTION**: Take 26 minutes to read designated chapter, question or comment. Y – YOU'RE IN SANE!
Are they servants of Christ? --I speak as if insane--I more so; in far more labors, in far more imprisonments, beaten times without number, often in danger of death. Five times I received from the Jews thirty-nine lashes. Three times I was beaten with rods, once I was STONED; three times I was shipwrecked, a night and a day I have spent in the deep. *Read more.* I have been on frequent journeys, in dangers from rivers, dangers from robbers, dangers from my countrymen, dangers from the Gentiles, dangers in the city, dangers in the wilderness, dangers on the sea, dangers among false brethren; I have been in labor and hardship, through   2 Corinthians 11:23-26

<u>JOURNALIZE AND POLISH YOUR PURPOSE:</u>

- Read the Beatitudes, Matthew 5:3-12 and Luke 6:20-24, Sermon on the MOUNT THAT Jesus blessed the disciples with.
- Write about a situation that you felt it nearly drove you insane. How did you handle it?

Please post the "Sermon on the Mount" on to the bathroom mirror and commit to memory to keep you in your sanity.

The BEATITUDES - HE said:

3 "Blessed are the poor in spirit,
    for theirs is the kingdom of heaven.
4 Blessed are those who mourn,
    for they will be comforted.
5 Blessed are the meek,
    for they will inherit the earth.
6 Blessed are those who hunger and thirst for righteousness,
    for they will be filled.
7 Blessed are the merciful,
    for they will be shown mercy.
8 Blessed are the pure in heart,
    for they will see God.
9 Blessed are the peacemakers,
    for they will be called children of God.
10 Blessed are those who are persecuted because of righteousness,
    for theirs is the kingdom of heaven.
11 Blessed are you when people insult you, persecute you and falsely say all kinds of evil against you because of me.
12 Rejoice and be glad, because great is your reward in heaven, for in the same way they persecuted the prophets who were before you.

Fish Hook Quote: Be Accountable and cognizant of your behavior here on earth,
On judgment day God may not accept your temporary insanity plea for acting like a jerk!
T. Cobb-Morgan

Chart of Manifestations

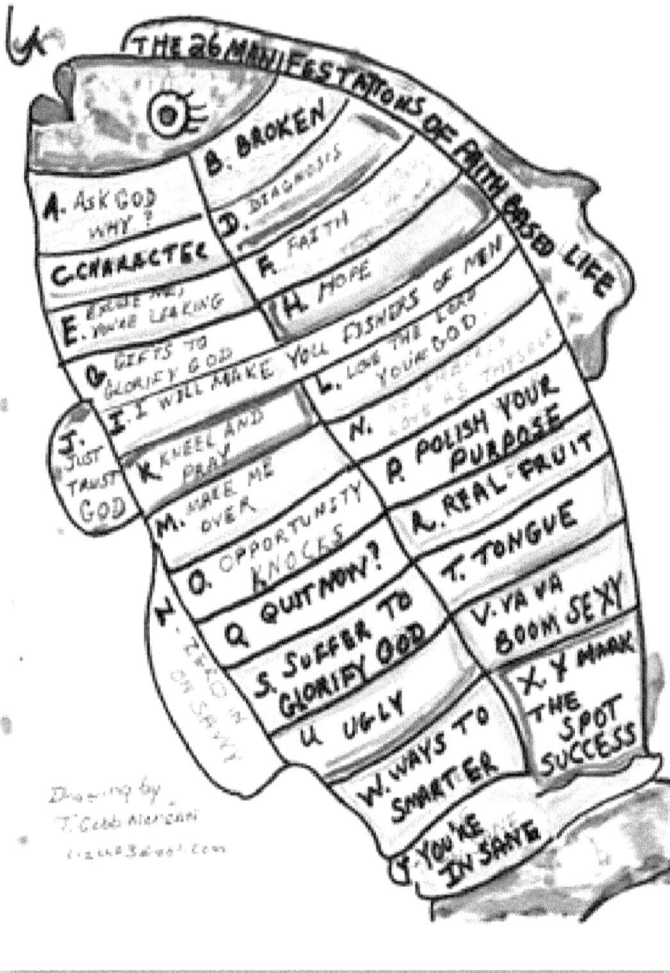

10

IS THERE A FISH DOCTOR IN THE HOUSE?
WJF - Real acts of goodness with the fruit of the spirit

R IVER WALKS ALONG the Fishing park embankment to the end of the pier. River yells for pink lady to respond as he anxiously looks for movement in the river. I'm not staying; I had to get my jacket! Where are you pink lady? Can you hear me?

Pink lady is faint and weak in voice. She slowly floats to the top. Her eyes are puffy and dilated. Her pink scales are loose, her skin is greasy and blackened and her gills are swollen.

River, are you there? She whispers.

He rushes to her, "Pink Lady, what happened?"

She coughs, let's just say I river-danced with a hungry Big Blue Heron bird. He insisted upon taking the lead.

River insists and convinces her to see a veterinarian! Listen, I'm going to transport you in my fishing cooler. I will add some river water to keep you in a natural nutrient-rich bath.

River, I'll be fine, as she glops river water, retreats Pink Lady. By, the way what is a veterinarian?

He explains, that's a fish doctor and she is my auntie.

She coughs AGAIN; all I need is a bowl of Minnow and seaweed soup, Kelp bath and a good night's rest. She falls asleep and River gingerly picks her up and heads for his Aunties office.

Pond,) Hey, are we really taking a wild big mouth bass to the doctor whispering and puzzled toward Pond.

Lake responds, ain't this a blip! I never saw a doctor except for the school nurse doing new Fall year school physicals. One year I remember running in the house from the city basketball courts with pieces of DNA missing! I got an alcohol rub down, two baby aspirin and vapor rub around my neck.

Pond questions, did it help?

Lake elaborates, WELL; I developed an awesome three pointers shot which I patented as the "Lucrative Lake" because no one would stand within ten feet of the menthol!

River, on his cell phone, Hello, is "Dr. Gaines in." Hey Auntie this is River. You have done a spectacular job in taking care of our dog Bear. Bear? He's fine. I have an unusual situation for you, a wild Big Mouth Bass fish. Yes, you heard me correctly. You do? You have a post graduate qualification in aquatic animal health. Great, may I meet you at the office? I'm ten minutes away.

Thank you for agreeing to meet me here. I have my pet bass, Pink Lady, with injuries. Can you help her?

Nephew, no problem, let's see what is going on. Did you have her outside in the direct sun? Her pink skin has darkened and it feels greasy. A couple of aloe drops will clear that right up. (She puts the drops in the fish mouth). She also has an extra deformed fin with an injury. Would you like for me to cut it off? (She turns around to get her scalpel).

Pink Lady's eyes pop open and she panics, pump your brakes Tuts… I'm out of here! How would you feel if I just cut one of your legs off?

By the way, they are sprouting hair. (She starts head butting the cooler container).

Dr. Auntie replies, I beg your pardon River? (As she turns around, she notices the fish moving)

River quickly clears his voice, OH; I was just clearing my throat.

(Pink Lady is still protesting by head butting the cooler container).

River, she is quite aggressive. Perhaps I can stabilize her with an injection. (She turns around to get a needle syringe.)

In disbelief, Pink Lady circles the cooler and angrily replies, AREN'T you a busy little thing with your collection of scalpels and needle arsenals. River, get me out of here before Dr. "Kill a Bass" filets me!

RIVER clears his voice again, ahem… Auntie, I have another appointment. Please bill me for the charges. Thank you, ma'am, it was a pleasure. I'll see you at the Engagement dinner.

(He heads out the door with Pink lady.)

Pink Lady, will you cool it when we are in the company of people? You almost gave yourself away!

Pink Lady glares him, Really River? I feel that my behavior was appropriate, considering that your "auntie" was trying to donate me to Science! Two more minutes in there and she would have had my parts headed for a high school biology class. My role would be dead fish in the petri dish experiment! (Exasperated) River, please take me home!

INT. RIVER'S PARENTS HOUSE - EVENING

River takes the fishing cooler back to his home to keep an eye on Pink Lady. He places the cooler in the bathtub and a wooden slat over it resembling a child's See/Saw toy. Exhausted, he sits down to watch Pink Lady as she is asleep. He notices tiny writing on her body. Wow, could it be a tattoo of? NO, WAY! Suddenly remembering the flower shop errand, he jumps up to head back out to the Flower shop to pick up samples.

River closes his room door and is in the house.

What a long day! Great, Pink Lady is sleeping. I'll just leave her in the bathtub and check on her later.

(AGAIN, He glances in the cooler in the bathtub. "What an awesome tattoo of the FRUIT OF THE SPIRIT!

Man, I still must go the flower shop to pick up the bouquet samples.

STOP and Reflect! To Work on WJF Worksheet, Journal and FOCUS at the end of each chapter or CONTINUE.

Manifestation end of chapter Ten
IS THERE A FISH DOCTOR IN THE HOUSE?
WJF - Real acts of goodness with the fruit of the spirit

PRAYER: Pray for 26 seconds on Topic of Focus - Biblical **Manifestation**:
R- Real acts of goodness with the fruit OF THE SPIRIT!
KEEP IN STEP WITH THE FRUIT OF THE SPIRIT! Galatians 5:22-26

DEVOTION: Take 26 minutes to read chapter and challenge question.
Keep in Step with the FRUIT OF THE Spirit
[22] But the fruit of the Spirit is love, joy, peace, patience, kindness, goodness, faithfulness, [23] gentleness, and Self-control; against such things there is no law. [24] And those who belong to Christ Jesus have crucified the flesh with its passions and desires. [25] If we live by the Spirit, let us also keep in step with the Spirit. [26] Let us not become conceited, provoking one another, envying one another. Galatians 5:22-26

R – REACH OUT TO OTHERS – FRUIT OF THE SPIRIT

JOURNALIZE AND POLISH YOUR PURPOSE:
Galatians 5:22-26 Commit to Memory

Fish Hook Quote: Be cognizant of your behavior here on earth,
On judgment day God may not accept your temporary insanity plea!
T. Cobb-Morgan

But the **fruit of the Spirit** is:

Love – Send God a love note through prayer and others via personal delivery.

Joy – Call an old friend and make them smile today!

Peace – Show others how to keep peace; talking disturbs the peace. (Don't FORGET TO OFFER "peace offerings" of homemade notes, candy and fresh picked flowers.)

Patience – Wait for it! Continue your lessons of impatience with others!

Kindness - TREAT someone to a free lunch!

Goodness – Practice Acts of Kindness daily.

Faithfulness – Till the end!

Gentleness – Especially when correcting children and pets!

Self-control – Especially when driving- stay away from road rage!

Fish Hook Quote:

> ***How can The Fruit of the Spirit be being real if it has,*** The Love of passionfruit, but non-nutritional needs?
> ***Is the Fruit of the Spirit real if it has?***
> The Joy of eating pomegranates but no VISIBLE SEEDS!
> ***Is the Fruit of the Spirit real if it has?***
> The Peace of eating a succulent peach but there is no juice running down my arms,
> ***Is the Fruit of the Spirit real if it has?***
> The Patience of eating a watermelon without the 100 seeded charms,
> ***Is the Fruit of the Spirit real if it has?***
> The Kindness of sharing strawberries but no fragrance in the air,
> ***Is the Fruit of the Spirit real if it has?***
> The Goodness of biting an apple but absent is the crunch.
> ***Is the Fruit of the Spirit real if it has?***
> The Faithfulness of munching grapes but no large juicy bunch

Is the Fruit of the Spirit real if it has?
The Gentleness of eating a banana, but no peeling to throw away,
Yes, the Fruit of the Spirit is real
And feeds me self-control to keep me abiding in HIS vine every day!

T. Cobb Morgan

11

HAVE WE MET?
WJF – Love the Lord With all Your Heart, Soul and Mind

R IVER APPROACHES THE Flower Shop door and notices a closed sign. He sees a clerk leaving the counter. River knocks at the door. Hey, Eileen, would you please open the door?

Michelle (clerk and Eileen's niece)

Michelle doesn't even look up. Sorry sir, we are closed.

Eileen, I'm river. You are expecting me to pick up the sample wedding bouquets. Please open the door.

Michelle looks over at Eileen to get her nod of approval to open the door. Eileen is in search of the bouquets behind the counter doors.

Michelle responds, just a minute I'm coming. She unlocks the door from inside with her key. She quickly feels her waist for Powder Blue Girl, her five-shot revolver. She knows Eileen holsters a Tiffany Collection, thigh Glock in Lilac she rocks! But she fears her Auntie would never use it!

Hi Eileen, I'm River. I see you run a tight ship here…lock down at 6:01 p.m.

Michelle mimics, save the "sorry I'm late" for Eileen. She is across the counter waiting for you.

Eileen is a natural beauty with a pleasant personality and savvy business acumen. Her beautiful smile IS AS RIGHT AS RAIN. SHE IS WEARING A COTTON DRESS WITH FLORAL PRINT AND A DENIM JACKET.

Eileen is on the other side of the counter with her head down pulling the last bouquet. (She is in a wheelchair usually at the end of the day due to leg fatigue. Most of the time she uses a cane).

I'm over here River, pulling the last bouquet.

River walks over to the counter. She looks up and their eyes lock. (The late Singer and Parkinson Survivor, Maurice White of Earth, Wind and Fire appear singing Love's Holiday.) They both smile as they awkwardly unlock glances.

Hi River, I'm Eileen by the way. What a pleasure to finally meet you. She extends her arm to shake hands.

River gently takes her hand in his and lightly kisses it. Eileen by the way I'm River and I assure you the pleasure is ALL mine.

Eileen smiles but keeps a business-like persona. My goodness, I have a charmer on my hands. Your fiancée is lucky lady. With I have a sample box of lucky 7 bouquets. You may take them home and advise your fiancée to return the bouquets within three business days. She may call me and here are a few of my business cards, if she has any questions. Good luck on your wedding. By the way, your brother came in to inquire on your order.

River clarifies, "My" brother, Carlos?

No, his name was not Carlos. He left his business card. (looks at card) Larkson Nedo.

Oh, that explains IT; he is my best friend and best man in my wedding. I owe him. He did me a huge favor and picked up my fiancée from the airport.

Eileen is puzzled as she recalls Larkson engaged in heavy KISSING WITH a woman in his car but she did not mention it to River.

River sorts out details to Eileen. He must have been checking on his lapel corsage. (Refocusing) Eileen, have we met? You look and sound so familiar. I noticed you are wearing military dog tags. Are they your husband's or your boyfriend's? They certainly could not be yours.

She corrects him, I beg your pardon? There is neither husband NOR BOYFRIEND. I spent an eight-year tour in the military as a medic outside of Afghanistan. I was sent home on disability for an injury to my leg which tires easily so I sit in the wheelchair.

Hoorah! As River chants his army greeting. I too served during most of the 2000's. Please forgive me for being presumptuous. Oh, I AM sorry about your leg injury.

No problem, as she reverts to BUSINESS. Anyway, I'd rather not discuss it. It was a stressful decade of my life.

Say no more, recants River. I understand. Sometimes I wonder why most of us veterans don't wear a PTSD sticker on our foreheads. By the way, did you go to school here? I manage a security team downtown at the club, "Green (ARMY) FRIENDS of Distinction". Have you been there for a visit?

No, I've been so busy with the flower shop. Besides, my clubbing' days are over.

I imagine you were hot on the dance floor...teasing River says err, UM maybe back in the day.

I beg your pardon? Challenges Eileen. Oh, I'm still hot. My wind down time now consists of a hot bubble bath, a hot old school cd, hot bourbon wings and a hot latte'. Call me SSS, Sister Still Sizzling! Honey, I may walk with cane but I'm no "fish out of water!"

River remembers, Oh my God! A fish out of water! Eileen thanks for the samples. We will be in touch. I've got to run to take care of a sick fish.

A what? She searches for a response.

Michelle approaches from the back. Auntie, you heard Don Juan correctly...a sick fish! That explains his cheesy pickup lines, unless, of course, he owns a fish nursery hatchery out in the Marina.

Too bad he's engaged, said Eileen. He is a babe in a quirky kind of way. If only we had met during a different time. I was too eager to trade my 20's for Uncle Sam's scenic tour in Afghanistan. Michelle, he's right. We have crossed paths, but I can't remember where, how or when. It's getting late, let's get out of here.

Meanwhile, River arrives at his parents' home and turns the key to open door.

Pond alarms uh oh. Do you smell fish frying?

Lake agrees and says, this can't be good.

Aunt Irene! (River frantically running into Kitchen) What are you doing?!

She smiles, hey River! Well, I'm fixing up a mess of bass fish for your Engagement dinner tonight. I remembered how much you like my creamed cornbread and it is in the oven. In fact, your Aunt Acara and Aunt Alesha just left to get changed. We finished the baked HAM, fried turkey, greens, mac & cheese, YAMS, peach cobbler and iced tea...and your FAVORITE DESSERT cake Devil's food chocolate with Cream cheese frosting! I've been kissing it off your face since you were two!

She offers A BEAUTIFUL tray to him.
Here, try one of my baked mushrooms stuffed with spinach dip.

Thanks Auntie, but what I need to know is where did you get the fish?

There was a big white cooler in the middle of the kitchen floor, she said.

Aunt Irene who went up to my room and took the liberty of removing my cooler?

What are you talking about dear? Your Uncle Ray dropped off the fish in his cooler. No one has been in your room…here Lady Gaga, come here girl.

(Lady Jana, a white Persian, cat is so full she comes wobbling in and burps! RIVER LOOKS AT HER STOMACH)

Oh no, Pink Lady! Are you in there yells RIVER?

Who is Pink Lady, asks Aunt Irene?

River races upstairs, I'll explain later.

He runs into the bedroom and approaches the white cooler in the bathtub.

She's gone. I'm too late.

(He backs into the wall and slides down to the floor.)

What have I done? How could I be so careless? She didn't deserve this. She was so full of life, a great dancer and a soulful songstress. More than anything, she was a good friend. I'd give anything to hear her voice again. HANGS HIS HEAD

Pink Lady calmly says, River?

Pink Lady? Is that you? Where are you?

Yes, I'm up here, on the shelf.

What are you doing up there?

Pink Lady snips sarcastically. Let's see, I was auditioning for a book-ends part, but since my twin didn't show up they passed over me.

However, I'll tell you who did show up... your Aunt's "Pesky catfish with hair" creature! He was trying to make me his lunch special. River, what do you think I'm doing up here? Get me down!

Amused, River empathizes, Sorry about that. I see you've met Auntie's cat, Lady Gaga. She's really a gentle cat and sweet as a kitten.

Save it for her Feline best seller biography and kitty cat memoirs, scoffs Pink Lady.

(RIVER GENTLY TAKES HER DOWN)

River insists, OKAY; let's get you hydrated right away Pink Lady. I will slowly immerse you back in the remaining water. Doesn't that feel better? The organic minnows in there are complements of Dr. Gaines the veterinarian. I must get ready for dinner. Delilah wants the family to hear her announcement. I was supposed to pick her up from the airport but she caught a ride with Lark.

A concerned Pink Lady voices, River, be careful around her. I don't trust her.

I am trying Pink Lady, assures River. I even talked to my best friend Lark but he didn't have much to say.

Pink Lady interrupts, you need to feed him with a long spoon too!

Pink Lady, what are you trying to say, Queries RIVER?

Pond blurts, Run fool! A big mouth bass is an awesome fish when it comes to assessing situations. Her basic senses; sight, taste, touch, smell and hearing are radar.

Lake chimes in, I agree. Their senses are magnified. Bass can detect variations and the PH in the sea. They are very aware of their surroundings. In other words, bass fish know what is lurking in the water bushes, if something spilled in the bay and if it is going to rain. She's a virtual swimming black box of information! In other words, she knows what time it is!

A relenting Pink Lady, let's discuss the details after dinner. By the way, be cool during dinner. Everything is going to work out in your favor according to the plan. I'd prefer you lock me in the car, far away from that furry catfish creature... It's been a long day and I need a nap without keeping one eye open.

Your wish is my command. (He puts her in the back of the van)

Pink lady is relaxing in River's van during late evening.

Wow, it is dark, cold and scary back here. These would be perfect conditions …at home. I'd be eating sea kelp chips and watching a Bass and Furious movie. Home Sweet Home is where I long to be, gasped Pink Lady.

The song, "Home Sweet Home is Where I Long to be" plays, written by T. Cobb Morgan.

HOME SWEET HOME IS WHERE I LONG TO BE
Written by T. Cobb Morgan – LizLL03@aol.com

Home, Sweet Home is where I long to be. (I can't wait to get there)

Home, SWEET HOME a place of tranquility. (Are you kidding?)

Craziness, laziness, all wrapped up in one. (Hey, CHARLIE'S bus is outside)

Yes dysfunction, no assumption, gee did we have fun! (Rhonda ask IF WE can ride to Buck roe Beach)

Home, Sweet, Home we kids made so much noise. (Our poor parents)

Our house the friends met, all the girls and boys. (Man, 29 Scotland was the place)

Every blue moon I ride by just to look and see, (In my red b210 hatchback)

To find my younger self waving back at me! (Does she have my earrings on?)

Craziness, laziness, all wrapped up in one. (PEANUT please make Crystal and June spaghettis.)

Yes dysfunction, no assumption, gee did we have fun! (Gainer you want government grill cheese, we are out of peanut butter and jelly.)

Home, Sweet, Home we grew up way too fast, (Someday will be together)

Had I known, I would have made it last.

Home, SWEET, HOME I must get off the phone, (Terry, your phone curfew is 9 p.m.)

Good night, tomorrow we will make memories of my own. (We may roam there is no place like home)

STOP to Reflect Work on WJF: Worksheet, Journal and FOCUS at the end of each chapter or CONTINUE.

Manifestation end of Chapter Eleven
Have We Met?
IN 26 DAYS! – love THE LORD YOUR god, WITH ALL YOUR HEART, and SOUL AND MIND.

PRAYER: Pray for 26 seconds on Topic of Focus - Biblical Manifestation: THE PARABLE OF THE GOOD SAMARITAN – LOVE THE LORD.

DEVOTION: TAKE 26 minutes to Luke26:28
READ DESIGNATED BOOK CHAPTER AND SCRIPTURE: ...26"WHAT IS WRITTEN IN THE LAW?" JESUS REPLIED. "HOW DO YOU READ IT?" 27HE ANSWERED, "' LOVE THE LORD YOUR GOD WITH ALL YOUR HEART AND WITH ALL YOUR SOUL AND WITH ALL YOUR STRENGTH AND WITH ALL YOUR MIND' AND 'LOVE YOUR NEIGHBOR AS YOURSELF.'" 28"YOU HAVE ANSWERED CORRECTLY," JESUS SAID. "DO THIS AND YOU WILL LIVE?" ...love THE LORD, YOUR GOD WITH ALL YOUR HEART, and SOUL AND MIND. Luke 10:26-28

JOURNALIZE AND POLISH YOUR PURPOSE: Explain why we must love God as part of our purpose.

Fish Hook Quote:

Whatever you believe in your HEART will take effect,
It will print on the SOUL and never reject,

> It may crush or build your spirit to neglect or respect
> What is in your heart, soul and spirit will manifest!

T. COBB MORGAN

Challenge Question One: When WAS your last HEART TALK WITH God?

Challenge Question TWO: Write a love letter to God.

Challenge Question THREE: Honor God with a Prayer of love.

God a Letter about:

"'LOVE THE LORD YOUR GOD WITH ALL YOUR HEART AND WITH ALL YOUR SOUL AND WITH ALL YOUR STRENGTH AND WITH ALL YOUR MIND'

12

GRANNIE HOG MA PLEASE!
WJF – Love Your Neighbor as Yourself

GRANNIE HOG MA, MG's mother, is looking for her pearl earrings to wear with her floral dress, glasses and a bag. SHE is helping Liz with the finishing touches to her dress.

Grannie Hog Ma, please help me with my blouse, pearls and some perfume.

I'm coming DEAR; rushes MG. Here's your evening dose and some water. We need to head downstairs as the guests are arriving and we need to be on time to greet them.

Grannie Hog Ma grunts, Snort, Snort, What the smell? Frog, I got this. The guests can wait. Beauty and perfection takes time. Just look at me. (She holds up a mirror and ax Murderer music plays, DUN DUN dun DAH!) She panics, OMG, quick get the tweezers! I have a wild hair!"

MG and LIZ (Looking puzzled) How can you tell?

Grannie Hog Ma REMARKS, because it's gray! I refuse to look old.

MG asks Liz, would you prefer to sit in your power chair or a regular dining CHAIR.

Liz asserted, Thanks. DOORBELL RINGS perhaps my wheel chair just in case I need to hurry off to the bathroom. I'm having some mild Parkinson's anxiety, my lower back hurts and I feel a headache coming on.

Aunt Aleshia, shouts Knock, knock. I'm here for the golden girl, excuse me, I mean Liz.

GRANNIE HOG MA calls MG, Frog, and (Looks at MG) Who Data? Snort, Snort. What the smell? I smell that Ba Dunk a Dunk Aleshia and two more folks.

Aleshia, Surprise! Hi Grannie Hog Ma. You remember my daughter Leslyen and her special friend British?

MA GRANNIE HOG, Well, hello "Lesbian" and "Skittish".

MG, Mother, that's Lesley and British. British is from London.

GRANNIE HOG MA says, here we go! We are losing another of our dirty south sweet potatoes bites to the British dust! Remember that Chiquita girl...

MG says, "Mama, her name is Lupita Nyong'o...she's from Africa."

GRANNIE HOG MA, Snort, Snort! What the smell! (Side eye glance) It's a pleasure to see all of you. I'm going home to pick up my banana pudding. May God bless and love you all! She sings Precious Lord On her way out.

LIZ ASKS, SIS, how long have you been standing there? AUNT ALESHIA REPLIES, long enough to hear that you are giving Parkinson's too much credit. MG, we have a plan. We refuse to let it ruin your evening. I will accommodate you to the powder room for discreet potty breaks, LaCara will fix your plate, Irene will administer your medications and Ray will pick up the slack. Now take a deep breath and let's enjoy River's engagement dinner. MG, please finish getting dressed; we will take good care of her.

MG SMILES AND COMMENTS,

I'm so blessed with wonderful siblings-in-law. Thanks, Aleshia!
FADE OUT

STOP! To Work on WJF: Worksheet, Journal and FOCUS at the end of each chapter or CONTINUE.

Manifestation end of Chapter Twelve grannie HOG MAW. Please! WJF – Neighborly Love for all people

PRAYER: Pray for 26 seconds on Topic of Focus - Biblical Manifestation: n – neighborly LOVE ALL PEOPLE AS THYSELF.

DEVOTION: Take 26 minutes to read chapter and challenge question. And the very God of peace sanctify you wholly; and *I pray God* your whole spirit and soul and body be preserved blameless unto the coming of our Lord Jesus Christ.
24 Faithful *is* he that called you, who also will do *it*.
25 Brethren, pray for us.
26 Greet all the brethren with a holy kiss.
27 I charge you by the Lord that this epistle is read unto all the holy brethren I Thessalonians 5:23-27

Question: who IS your NEIGHBOR?
Answer: all people

JOURNALIZE Explain the following Passage;
29Jesus answered, "The foremost is, 'HEAR, O ISRAEL! THE LORD OUR GOD IS ONE LORD; 30AND YOU SHALL LOVE THE LORD YOUR GOD WITH ALL YOUR HEART, AND WITH ALL YOUR SOUL, AND WITH ALL YOUR MIND, AND WITH ALL YOUR STRENGTH.' 31"The second is THIS; 'YOU SHALL LOVE YOUR NEIGHBOR AS YOURSELF.' There is no other command-ment greater than these."

POLISH YOUR PURPOSE: Explain THE OLD SAYING, "to HAVE A FRIEND YOU must be A FRIEND." How do you show friendship?

Fish Hook Quote: Love by God's commandment until you ae able to do it on your own.
T. COBB MORGAN

Journal Page for Chapter 12

13

THE ENGAGEMENT DINNER, ELDER COBB PLEASE BLESS THE FOOD
WJF- Broken

(DINNER IS DONE Screenplay Style)
LIZ
Good evening everyone!
FAMILY
Good evening!
(MG ARRIVES FIVE MINUTES LATER)
MG
Welcome our Dear Family and Friends. We are delighted that you have joined us tonight to celebrate River and Delilah's engagement. Elder Cobb, Pop, will you do the honors and bless our meal?

(Liz narrates "My Dad's Footsteps, as her father prays to ask God's blessing upon the meal.)
MY DAD'S FOOTSTEPS, poem written by T. Cobb Morgan
LizLL03@aol.com

My DAD'S WALK is His Mouthpiece – Listen to His Steps!
My Dad's profession was that of a master welder,

His footsteps could be heard getting ready for work,

He was always on time; grabs his coffee and LUNCH HIS steps of responsibility he'd never shirk.

I can hear him step up into his 57 Chevy truck cranking down the road waving at the neighbors as he passed their way,

"Hey Mr. C, are the greens in your garden ready or may I borrow your riding mower today?

The greens need a few more weeks and because he didn't want his things broken, "I'll help you" his steps of assistance would say.

When those greens graced the table, Pop's blessing would be so long,

We teased that the greens are cold again, we were so wrong!

You see my dad didn't like things or people broken, and upon meeting them he stepped to repair them as new,

He would then give them new purpose with a welding solder or mentor them from the book of life with a scripture or two.

Either way he would step to pray for them that they would choose a relationship with their Lord and Savior Jesus Christ,

Because he knew Psalm 37:23 states, "**The steps of a good man are ordered by the LORD, and He will surely bless your life.**

River glances over at Pop and remembers POP as,

I remember my Pop and our family always made a way,

My mom was taking me to daycare and Pop said not today.

Give me that baby boy, I take issue, he's too young to be away,

Take the time, teach him the word of God, his soul will never STRAY.

My Pop is a godly man, a baseball fan, a bible believer too, a shipyard welder, a gracious Elder and a friend to all of you.

He stands tall at 5'5, strong as fierce as a lion,
Never worked out in a gym, never pumped weights of iron,
Keen as an eagle, and gentle as a dove,
Brave as a military soldier always showed God's love.
My Pop is a godly man, a baseball fan, a bible believer too, a
shipyard welder, a gracious Elder and a friend to all of you.

LIZ (Voiceover), I will always love my Dad and will always try to walk in his footsteps. (Her poem v/o as He prays)

ELDER COBB (LIZ'S FATHER) let us bow our heads. Heavenly Father, we thank you for this wonderful meal we are about to receive for the nourishment of our bodies. In Jesus name, we pray. Amen!

The Family ends grace, Amen! (THE FAMILY STARTS EATING)

AUNT ALESHIA questions Mark, why are you eating Aunt Ivy's famous pound first?

Life is SHORT; eat Aunt Ivy's Pound Cake dessert first!

AUNT IVY looks around the room and says, "Eat up everybody. I have plenty of desserts: Pound cake with icing variations almond, chocolate and caramel, Pecan Tarts and Butter cookies!"

CARLOS (RIVER'S BROTHER)

(END OF MEAL) Here, here family and friends, may I please have your attention? Let's raise a toast to River and Delilah!

DELILAH interrupts, excuse me please, I have something to say. Uh River, I am sorry I can't marry you. SHE GIVES HIM THE RING.

DINNER GUESTS Breath gasps circle the room, followed by silence.

RIVER gulps, I beg your pardon? What are you really saying Delilah?

DELILAH nonchalantly answers, it's complicated. But in a nutshell, Lark and I are in love. We are getting married and moving to Florida.

RIVER glares, Lark who? You mean my best friend since 7th grade Larkson Anthony Nedo? Man, is this TRUE?

LARK tries to LOOK SINCERE; yeah man…I'm sorry dawg.

RIVER, yes you are. PAUSE FAMILY; please join me in raising a toast to Larkson and Delilah. May your union last and prove you two truly deserve each other.

Having said that, I want to thank you all for coming and have a goodnight family, I love you all. But right now, I need some fresh air.

FAMILY empathetically responds, Good-bye River.

RIVER, Goodnight! Mom and DAD please don't wait up for me. He slams the door. Carlos, thanks for the toast and you should thank God that you have a wife like Kelicia.

DINNER GUESTS, (Comments heard in the room.) Oh, my God. Is this a prank? What just happened? I didn't see that coming! I need a stiff "drank!"

AUNT IRENE, mascara running down her face, I need a drink too! That woman! His friend is just as bad! They deserve each other. What a devious pair. She's scandalous trash and he is driving her trash truck! (Side eyes Delilah and Larkson.)

DELILAH

(She Yanks on Lark's sports jacket.) Lark, *I* think we should leave.

FADE OUT

STOP and Reflect! To Work on WJF Worksheet, Journal and FOCUS at the end of each chapter or CONTINUE.

Manifestation end of Chapter THIRTEEN
THE Engagement dinner
WJF- Broken

PRAYER: Pray for 26 seconds on Topic of Focus - Biblical Manifestation: broken

DEVOTION: TAKE 26 minutes to read designated chapter, question or comment.

Romans 11:17-27

B – BROKEN

Question: How can my broken body, soul and spirit be restored back to God?

Answer: God has the love and power to "graft" you back to HIM.
[17] But if some of the branches were broken off, and you, although a wild olive shoot, were grafted in among the others and now share in the nourishing ROOT [a] of the olive tree, [18] do not be arrogant toward the branches. If you are, remember it is not you who support the root, but the root that supports you. [19] Then you will say, "Branches were broken off so that I might be grafted in." [20] That is true. They were broken off because of their unbelief, but you stand fast through faith. So, do not become proud, but fear. [21] For if God did not spare the natural branches, neither will he spare you. [22] Note then the kindness and the severity of God: severity toward those who have fallen, but God's kindness to you,

provided you continue in his kindness. Otherwise you too will be cut off. [23] And even they, if they do not continue in their unbelief, will be grafted in, for God has the power to graft them in again. How much more will these, the natural branches, be grafted back into their own olive tree. **25**I do not want you to be ignorant of this mystery, brothers and sisters, so that you may not be conceited: Israel has experienced a hardening in part until the full number of the Gentiles has come in, **26**and in this way all Israel will be saved. As it is written: "The deliverer will come from Zion; he will turn godlessness away from Jacob. **27**and this is my covenant with them when I take away their sins."[g]   Romans 11:17-27

JOURNALIZE AND POLISH YOUR PURPOSE: What situation in life left you broken?

Fish Hook Quote:
   Broken

   My body was broken and God said Heal as new,
   My Soul was broken and God said restore as new,
   My spirit was broken and God
   Said refresh as new,
   And God said it be great to hear from you sometimes when nothing is Broken on you.

T. Cobb Morgan

14

EVERYBODY FREEZE THIS IS A STICK UP!
WFJ - Ugly

(DINNER CONTINUES SCREENPLAY Style) Artie - Villain ONE (Brandishing a gun) you're not going anywhere. Alright everybody put your hands up! Put all your money and valuables in the bag A/C pass the bag around.

A/C – Villain sniffles. Sure.

ARTIE Frowns, are you crying?

A/C, No I'm not crying, but you must admit it was so sad seeing River getting dumped. He LOOKS AT LARK AND DELILAH. You are just a low down scandalous pair of bird poop!

AUNT ALESHIA scoffs, you can say that again.

GRANDMA JEANNETTE prays, Amen to that.

ARTIE, all of you, shut-up!

CHRISTIAN (AGE 6), you're not supposed to say shut-up. You're supposed to say be quiet.

MG, angrily, who are you people? HE TURNS AROUND. Delilah is this your family?

DELILAH says, are you kidding me?

A/C proudly declares. We are the A/C bandits. We scope out your home while servicing your air conditioner unit. Then we come back and rob you.

ARTIE in disbelief yells, Miriam, stop talking!

FAMILY laughs, Miriam?!

SEAN (AGE 8), Miriam, you're going to jail.

ARTIE replies, Look, put these folks in the living room and put the little monsters in the room beside them in case we need a hostage.

AUNT LACARA, how dare you! Brother, you need to chill. White Boy Let me make you a prescription RX Long Island Iced Tea! Just what the doctor orders. Believe ME; I should know BECAUSE I'm married to one. Anyway, let's dance! You better start running like the dance the "Running Man! C'mon try it Miriam.

A/C, don't mind if I do! Sings, Girl, you got me running, singing Lenny Williams, oh, oh, oh, oh running!

ARTIE shouts, A/C!!! Look Lady don't test me. A/C Keep an eye on this group while I case the joint for additional valuables. If anybody tries anything…shoot them! Hey, you, Big Guy, (Looking at Larkson) COME with me.

LARKSON

Who? Me?

ARTIE

Yes you! I might need you to move some heavy furniture around to find some things.

LARKSON

Okay, just take it easy…and quit waving that gun in my face!

DELILA panics, oh no, Larkson, don't go! But leave your check-book, ATM card and gold tooth hidden in your SOCK IN case something goes down.

AUNT IRENE, I told she's a gold digger!

ARTIE Get upstairs. Move it or your dead meat!

THEY GO UPSTAIRS.

LARKSON, Good job Artie. Now we must work fast so they won't get suspicious and find out I'm involved with the robbery. Now empty the jeweler dresser while I look for the safe.

ARTIE questions, a safe?

LARKSON, Yes, behind the Black Madonna picture. Mrs. Bass painted it in high school back in the 1970's. She named her "My Beautiful Noir Madonna" aka her deceased mother, Sarah Belle and unborn child Darius.

ARTIE, WHAT? A Black Madonna? Even I know they were white.

LARKSON

Not quite. The original Black Madonna represented the statues and paintings of <u>Mary</u> and Baby Jesus. Over in Europe all her pictures show dark skin with black features. Michelangelo was commissioned by Pope Julius II to paint her white. Alright Artie, your history lesson is over. Crack the safe! (He pulls the picture frame open revealing the safe.)

Artie stretches his fingers and cracks his knuckles. He puts his ear to the wall and listens carefully as he cracks the safe, "CLICK".

LARKSON, excited, what a beautiful sound. Oh, I'll need some paper towels from the bathroom just in case they laced this safe with dye packets

ARTIE obliges, OH? Okay, but don't start without me.

LARKSON remarks, I wouldn't dare. Artie advances toward the bathroom. Larkson quickly puts on disposable gloves from his pocket and pulls a briefcase from under the bed. He pulls out money from the safe to stash in the briefcase. He runs over to the window and drops the suitcase into the flower bed gripping the gloves off with his teeth he puts them back in his pocket as Artie enters room. In a pretentious wait Larkson asks Artie, what took you so long?

ARTIE explains I had to take a leak. Here are the paper towels.

LARKSON inspects the safe but finds nothing but important papers. He wipes off his fingerprints, but sets artie up for his fingerprints to show up.

Hey Artie, there are only insurance policy papers. But check behind me as he hands him the papers.

ARTIE, disappointed, snipes nothing!

LARKSON trying to look concerned comments, really? LARKSON stole the ring but gives Artie hope, well, take out the jewelry and stash it into your pockets. *Be sure to get the Jamaican Black Pearl*, Mrs. Bass Mother's ring – very valuable. Her father won it in a semi-professional boxing match. Now quickly help me tie myself up so they won't suspect anything.

Artie agrees to the plan, sure thing! He ties up larkson and heads downstairs.

Meanwhile the energetic bad bass kids are getting restless. Milani, age four, jumps up on the table and crack! Her jump rope sounds like a whip.

Listen up you boy cousin morons! We need to come up with a plan to save ourselves. Any ideas?

CHRISTIAN sulked, I wish River was here. He would tell us what to do!

DUSTIN all our calls are going to his voicemail.

Milani reprimands, C'mon, THINK!

DUSTIN, age ten, comments, Ok Milani, here's the plan. Listen. Milani, Sean and Christian, this calls for Operation Cayenne Pepper Balloon the Baboons. I have an idea to take these guys down but we must work fast! Sean, booby trap the doorway when the other bandit comes back down he will trip over it.

He needed a few seconds to process the information as would any young man. Now, is "booby trap" the sling shot like fabric his mom looks for in the dryer on Monday morning she's avoided all weekend that some grown-ups refer to as a bra? Or is it the spy equipment he sees on the Pink Panther reruns on Saturday morning? His gut says "B", and SEAN grins, okay, Roger that.

Then, CHRISTIAN questions, "Who is Roger?"

DUSTIN advises CHRISTIAN; "ROGER" is our secret code confirmation. Now get out of the sleeping bag and prop it with Nana's sofa pillows to look like we are napping.

CHRISTIAN, I don't have to fake it – It's time for my naptime and I need a nap. Mommy!

Good grief, ok, says Dustin. Just stay the course! Never mind the time. This calls for action. Milani, get the hot water balloons ready with the special ingredient.

MILANI, chewing gum, pops a bubble and says, "I'm already on it!" She pulls out cayenne pepper from her jacket.

Dustin adds, listen gang, I'll pretend I must go to the bathroom but will be under the dining room table calling the police. After your missions are complete, meet me under the dining room table for further instructions.

ARTIE comes running downstairs.

Hey, we hit the jack-pot. WHOA!

(He trips over the rope and lands on the floor on his back.)

A/C bends down and looks at Artie nose to nose. Artie, are you alright?

ARTIE painfully responds, no you idiot, those brats got me freaking flat on my back! I thought those brats were asleep. Get me up! We got to get out of here!

Milani hollers, not so fast you broke down two bit pilferers! Fellas, take your positions super heroes!

Hit them high and hit them low.

Aim your HOT Water and hot pepper balloons and let them GO!

(Children hurl a barrage of Hot Water balloons towards the villains)

ARTIE, wrecking objects within his path, why you little monsters – the balloon bombs are burning my eyes!

(A/C rubbing his eyes) My eyes are burning too! Bad kids, bad kids!

(THEY RUN OUT BACKDOOR RIGHT INTO GRANNIE HOG MA).

GRANNIE HOG MA, Snort, snort. What the smell? Excuse yourselves for running into me. I almost dropped my Banana Pudding pies!

ROBBERS, Get out of the way.....

HOUSE GUEST, whatever you call her, don't call her...

ROBBER tells them to SHUT-UP! Get over there, old lady!

Sean, uh, oh! Run for cover, he called Grannie Hog Ma, old!

GRANNIE HOG MA –Snort. What the smell? Who are you two bit crooks calling old lady?!) She starts singing, Precious Lord take my hand; forgive me where these pies may land!

I am tired, (SHE shoves the pies in their faces), I am weak (head buts them) and I am worn.

Now where's cops, where's the heat, where the guys who walk the street are, take this 2-bit trash off my STREET...lead me home on. (She releases them and they run to police).   Down the Bass Driveway.

Policeman AND POLICEWOMAN, Freeze! Throw your weapons down, put your hands in the air and slowly walk backwards towards us!

A/C yells out at the Officers and confesses, "No problem officers, the weapons are fake."

Artie snaps at Miriam, shut-up!

Policeman and Policewoman, smile Miriam?! (THEY WRITE UP POLICE REPORT AS TOW TRUCK HAULS THE BANDITS VAN AWAY.)

A/C begs, Officer, I 'll do anything. Just get me away from that bearded lady! The POLICEMAN says what bearded lady? They turn around slowly and widen their eyes to their dismay and to their surprise stands Grannie hog maw five feet tall in size. Grannie Hog Maw is that you? What are you doing here? I haven't seen you down at precinct LATELY; I trust you are behaving yourself?

GRANNIE HOG MA, Is Bingo night on Wednesday? She flips her hair and sachets away).

POLICEMAN Looking at his partner. Wait a minute, didn't she tell Judge Hawkins she couldn't do children's community service on Wednesdays because of bible study/prayer meeting?

The Policeman says Yes sir. May I suggest they are probably better off?

Other policemen say you're probably right. Never mind! Anyway, you folks have a good day.

MG and guests arrive tired back into the house. I trust all of you have had enough excitement for one day.

HOUSE GUESTS answer Yes! You can say that again. Lord have mercy.

MG clears his throat, Ah hem! Lark and Delilah, don't you two have a plane to catch?

Lark replies, Yes Sir. We were just getting ready to say good-bye. Oh, and thanks for untying me from the chair. I'm glad they caught the robbers.

House Guests anxious to see them leave, Good bye! Good Riddance! Adios Amigos!

Guests remaining walk back into the house.

Larkson and Delilah jump into car and stop ahead at the flower garden.

Larkson looks at Delilah and tells he, I need TO CHECK my back tire…feels like it's losing air pressure. Also, I must check to see if I have a spare.

HE Gets out of the car and quickly pulls the briefcase out of the tall flowers bed and puts it in the trunk under the rug of the lower trunk. Nobody notices him, Delilah is putting on her lipstick and the guests have returned to the house. They drive off.

FADE OUT

STOP and Reflect! To Work on WJF Worksheet, Journal and FOCUS at the end of this chapter or CONTINUE.

Manifestation end of Chapter FOURTEEN - Everybody freeze this IS a Stick-up!
WFJ! - Ugly

PRAYER: Pray for 26 seconds on Topic of Focus - Biblical Manifestation: UGLY

DEVOTION: Take 26 minutes to read designated chapter, question or comment.
I believe ugly is as ugly does. That is, when we SIN. We choose to be ugly by taking an opportunity to sin. We must be like David and prepare to win, by asking God for forgiveness and truly giving in.

1 (*A Psalm* of David Psalm 26:1-5) Judge me, O LORD; for I have walked in mine integrity: I have trusted also in the LORD; *therefore,* I shall not slide.
2 Examine me, O LORD, and prove me; try my reins and my heart.
3 For thy lovingkindness *is* before mine eyes: and I have walked in thy truth.
4 I have not sat with vain PERSONS; neither will I go in with dissemblers.
5 I have hated the congregation of evil doers; and will not sit with the wicked.

Question: When we take on sin why does it spread over us more quickly than doing well?

Answer: First, let me say never be weary in well doing. Galatians 6:9King James Version (KJV)

[9] And let us not be weary in well doing: for in due season we shall reap, if we faint not.

So continue in good deeds and sow good seeds **Matthew 5:16** - Let your light so shine before men, that they may see your good works, and glorify your Father which is in heaven. Also sin seems to be more rampant because it seeps into our natural body, our soul (Mind, will and emotions) and the spirit as it flows through the heart.

JOURNALIZE AND POLISH YOUR PURPOSE: What are your spiritually UGLY setbacks that you are working on?

Fish Hook Quote:

> Ugly is as ugly does,
> That's what they say.
> Ugly is as ugly does,
> Got nothing to do with looks,
> Ugly is as ugly does,
> It is sin; find it in the good book,
> Ugly is as ugly does,
> Beauty quickly fades away,
> Ugly is as ugly does,
> That's what they say.
> Gray takes over, muscles ache
> AND THE MIND CAN'T RECALL THE DATE.

Ugly is as ugly does,
That's what they say.
You hurt FOR NO REASON, YOUR KNEES PREDICT
THE RAIN. EVERYTHING ON YOU IS IN PAIN.
Ugly is as ugly does, here comes the rain forgot my umbrella again,
Ugly is as Ugly DOES, what time is it again?

T. Cobb Morgan

15

A GAME OF SPADES ANYONE?
WJF – Zero in on Savvy

IT HAS BEEN a full day at the Bass Residence. However, Aunt Aleshia comments, well, the evening is still young. We have had a wonderful meal, an announcement of a broken engagement by the way, my money is on that breakup to be a mixed blessing. Please don't even mention the armed robbery. What is there left to do?

The House guests reply in unison, Let's Play Spades!

All seem to be in agreement except for one voice of reason, the mascot and score keeper with a vengeance, Aunt Gainer. She is also Dr. Gainer and the youngest sister of the Bass household. As a little girl, she always has a way with animals and cared for them with homemade sugar cube placebos, cut up washcloths for gauze and even soda cubes for upset stomachs…until Aunt Mary Jane aka "Phrewinch" found out her colas were missing!

She threw up her hands in surrender and got back to the business at hand, policing spade games. Listen family, again, no cheating. According to Spades Handbook for Nut Jobs here are the rules.

House Guests reply, Nut Jobs! Who?

Quiet please. In the Spades for handbook, it says this game is played among couples, partners or pairs. You all should be familiar with the bidding process. The book starts from the highest and down to lowest: Ace, King, Queen, Jack, Ten, 9, 8, 7, 6, 5, 4, 3 and 2.

Aunt Aleshia, ADJUSTING HER CARDS HAT AND GLASSES alerts, (Sarcastically) ahem, "Dr. Gainter" emergency call in the kitchen for you. It appears some dignitary in Peach Tree Groves Estates needs assistance regarding SERVICES FOR a pet to spade or neuter? (Gainer jumps up and grabs her veterinarian bag.) I hate to send her on a wild goose chase in the damp weather, but she is putting a damper on my spades game that hasn't even started!

One of the Bad Bass grandchildren corrects Auntie. 'Aunt Aleshia, the term IS "spay" or neuter."

An hour later Gainer comes back. "It SEEMS THERE has been a false alarm regarding my services. Where are we in the game? I was hoping to direct the "shuffle and deal" process; of a 52-card deck making sure each card went out to each person playing has 13 cards."

Aunt Aleshia rubs her head, do we have any more refreshments? Lacara snapped, since when do you regard a bottle of Mascoutah as refreshments? Better yet, do we have a box on tap?

"Shut the front door," exclaims Lacara, the self-proclaimed Bass Family Bar Fly Apple Martini maker. It's in the fridge …grab an extra glass. This playing by the rules stuff is making me thirsty. You Hoo, Gainer, are you finished?

MILANI (4-Year-old granddaughter of Me Ma LaCara)

Me Ma, may I have this? (She is under the card table holding the "Queen of Spades" card which is different from her Old Maid cards.

AUNT LA CARA impatiently blurts, not now Milani. Me Ma am busy. Go get your bike and take your cards for a ride!

MILANI (PUTS THE CARD IN HER TOY PURSE) AND chimes OK Me Ma, bye-bye!

Gainer, with bull horn and handbook in hand, "Ok team, I just had a false alarm. Try to lead out with lowest to highest clubs, hearts or diamonds."

Aunt Irene, GRABS HANDBOOK, let's hurry this along! Gainer please "can", "ditch" "trash the card maneuvers. I feel a migraine coming on - Give me that. Hey where is the little girl we paid to call Gainer from upstairs?

Gainer, What?!

Aunt Lacara, annoyed, yells out. Shuffle and bid! Besides, everybody knows, we call Grannie Hog Ma for Spade maneuvers and her Banana Cream Pies!

Aunt Aleshia says, "Yummy that sounds good. I'll open with five or six books."

Gainer asks, what are you leading?

Aunt Aleshia snips don't worry about it. Bid.

I'll take three.

I'll jump in. adds Aleshia

Aunt LaCara, grunts and yawns out loud. Is there any more chicken?

Don't be greasing up the cards! Warns Lacara.

Aleshia remembers, anybody check on Liz?

Yes, she's in bed working on her Parkinson's screenplay, adds Lacara. Said she was making dopamine in her brain. She's trying to get other Parkinson survivors works on her bandwagon. Muhammed Ali's daughter, Michael. Fox, Linda Ronstadt and other survivors to back up her voice of advocacy by appearing in her movie! Sadly, Maurice White and The Greatest, Ali, passed away.

You know I'm usually not the one to put a damper on things but our sister Liz has always been a big dreamer, says Aunt Aleshia. Some people wonder if she's being realistic. Or, maybe experiencing some delusions of grandeur?

MG (STANDING IN DOORWAY BEHIND), Interrupts, Take the edge off Aleshia and disregard "SOME PEOPLE", Come on Aleshia," She's happy. I think what's important is that we support her dreams and ambitions to succeed and leave a legacy for her family. Especially while she struggles through this disease. She may have changed a little on the outside with challenges of gait and posture, but her spirit is strong, her will is resilient and her mind is sharp and persistent.

MG, I truly admire you, smiles Gainer.

MG with remorse, thanks, but I've made mistakes. As her husband, friend and caregiver I'm only fulfilling my promise of "in sickness or in health." I truly draw from her strength and I ask God to heal her every day.

A smiling auntie chimes in, "How beautiful. He reminds me of my second husband Jeffrey, all religious and stuff."

Auntie Irene blurts, "leave the table MG. Cause I'm not trying to hear about her Jeffrey." He used to wear his wife beater undershirts to the family barbeques thinking he was Jeffrey Osbourne singing to the tune, "You should be mine."

And he woo, woo, woo,

Stole the good beers too

Never could deny a brew.

Wished they were mine, all twenty-nine!

You just got it twisted with your 3rd common law hubby "Heath Keep a SWEAT -Y Jerri curl, snips Aleshia.

Aunt Lacara, altos, (Leaning in IRENE ear mimic Artist Twisting lyrics.) Baby, baby I know, Baby, I love you so,

You, Jada, Tracee, Chantal and Mary Jo!

Gainer asks, what ever happened to him?

We don't know. And... You don't want to know. It remains a mystery to this day.

GAINER questions, a mystery?

AUNT IRENE winks Yeah. A mystery to us too that he thought he could get beer muscles and raise his hand at us sisters looking for your Aunt Irene. He found out with the quickness that if he raised his hand at Aunt ALESHIA "He better be asking a question!'

GAINER readjusts, never mind. I have a feeling that mystery lesson just turned into a history lesson! Someone must be left behind to tell the story.

Aunt Aleshia remarks, "That Crepe Myrtle in her yard is bordered by a round concrete slab, pushing up Daisies."

Gainer covers her ears and tells them to stop incriminating. Alright ladies show your hands! I'll renege. Where is the Queen of Spades? I knew it! You all are cheating again! The Spades handbook for nut jobs rules was totally obsolete to you.

Wait a minute, scoffs LaCara. We are going to strip down, remove hats, take off wigs, remove shoes and overturn this table. The Queen of Spades is coming home tonight.

Someone needs to dial 911, says Aunt Lacara queries, why is that?

Aunt Irene smirks, why? It would be a crime to see you all naked. Heads of hair under those wigs laden with "Come Back Hair" grease would be looking like plucked chickens, thighs shaking like gelatin and toenails looking like corn chips! SPADE PLAYERS, where is the Queen-of-Spade?

Meanwhile, Miss Milani is putting the queen-of-spades card beside her old maid card on her back-wheel spokes with a clothes pin and takes off on her bike in the backyard. She stops to look at her cousin Kween Amaya and girlfriend EVonne toward Alex and "White boy" O'Hara. (Song: Kween AMAYA Written by T. Cobb Morgan)

Alex flirts, what's up Evonne …. Amaya. KWVONNE, when are you going out with me girl?

Evonne rolls her side eye, you could call a sistah.

WHITE BOY O'Hara awkwardly stumbles and regains is composure, Yeah Amaya, my queen, when are going to get with me, White boy O'Hara, a real brottha and King. Why won't you take my calls? Don't wait until I am distinguished, rich and successful University of Notre Dame graduate and Wall Street visionary.

AMAYA, swings her braids and articulates, stop calling me collect White Boy. Besides, I have dreams too. I want to graduate, study law, re-invent me and become a successful attorney.

WHITE BOY O'HARE (Takes her by the hand and whispers), "Keep my spot open …see you in ten years, we will be the talk of the class reunion. He lightly kisses her. Bye Amaya. (The boys turn down a different path and keep walking.)

KEVONNE, see you later girl, are you alright? Don't forget to study for Debate Team.

AMAYA, I don't know. I'm frozen from White Boy's kiss. (She glances down the road and White Boy O'Hara turns around and winks at her. She returns a smile). (Dazed) Okay, I'll bring my law book.

AMAYA IS sitting on a blanket meditating with candles, perfume oils and fruit.

Hi Kween Amaya. May I join your evening picnic? Approaches Milani.

KWEEN AMAYA embraces her, Hi Princess Milani. This is not a picnic. I'm MEDITATING upon my altar for peace. I enjoy getting away from Jamaica to spend my summers with Aunt Liz and Uncle MG. River even helped me with an internship. What are you doing?

MILANI, I have a busy schedule too! I'm Nana Liz's trusted courier and I'm taking the Queen and Old Maid for a ride! Don't take too much MEDICATION on your PEACH; it's not good for you.

KWEEN AMAYA (She laughs), SO proud of my little cousin, princess Milani. As Kween Amaya, I have some words of advice on royalty.

Hanging out with the Queen is customary,

But if you really want to know the shenanigans of the palace, (yelling heard from the house).

Hanging out with the Princess is legendary! (Milani bike spokes sport Queen of Spades}

FADE OUT

KWEEN AMAYA, written by T. Cobb Morgan

KWEEN AMAYA, she stands six feet tall.
KWEEN AMAYA, The harder the fall.
KWEEN AMAYA, Lives for today.
KWEEN AMAYA, she has to find her own way.
KWEEN AMAYA, she goes through life with a smile
KWEEN AMAYA, Positive is her child
KWEEN AMAYA, Learn for today
KWEEN AMAYA, she's must find her own way.
KWEEN AMAYA, she starts with a meditative spirit
KWEEN AMAYA, get close enough to hear it.
KWEEN AMAYA, knows for today
KWEEN AMAYA, she must find her own way.
KWEEN AMAYA, she wants a career of Politics,
KWEEN AMAYA, she must stand clear of legal zits!
KWEEN AMAYA, she must find her own way
KWEEN AMAYA, In a big, bold way.
KWEEN AMAYA, Knows for today,
KWEEN AMAYA, An ole KWEEN AMAYA,
KWEEN AMAYA gotta find her own way!

KWEEN AMAYA, Gone Girl
KWEEN AMAYA, Do your twirl
KWEEN AMAYA, Find Your Place in this world.

STOP and Reflect! To Work on WJF Worksheet, Journal and FOCUS at the end of this chapter or CONTINUE.

Manifestation end of Chapter Fifteen
WJF - Zero in on Savvy

PRAYER: Pray for 26 seconds on Topic of Focus - Biblical Manifestation: Savvy Z – zero in on Savvy

DEVOTION: Take 26 minutes to read designated chapter, Luke 18:1-6 for meditation or group discussion.

Z- Zero in BEING SAVVY
Key Scripture: Luke 18:1-6 (NIV)
The Parable of the Persistent Widow
18 Then Jesus told his disciples a parable to show them that they should always pray and not give up.
2 He said: "In a certain town there was a judge who neither feared God nor cared what people thought. 3 And there was a widow in that town that kept coming to him with the plea, 'Grant me justice against my adversary.'
4 "For some time he refused. But finally, he said to himself, 'Even though I don't fear God or care what people think, 5 yet because this widow keeps bothering me, I will see that she gets justice, so that she won't eventually come and attack me!'"
6 Question One: In the above scripture, what did Jesus tell the disciples regarding prayer and persistence?

Jesus said, we should always pray and never give up.

Question Two: What have you been praying for lately?

Write about a situation that you exercised savviness to fix it:

Fish hook quote:

> Dear Lord, may my prayers NOT be met with wait or NO's of resistance.
> He said to get a "YES"
> Pray and exercise savviness with Persistence.

Journal Notes:

16

GIMME THAT BALL!
WJF – Gifts to Glorify God

THE OUTDOOR VIRGINIA air smells clean and fresh after the warm fall shower. The tall pines start to shed their fragrant pine needles. and the honeysuckle tastes as sweet as it withers away with the fall season. The basketball court is a little slippery, but not too slippery for the. bad Bass grandkids. They welcome challenges with anything and enjoy the never-ending competition. Among their group, their mothers were delighted and relieved to hear the rain end and glad to see them go back outside. They are loud, rambunctious and skilled junior players. All dream of the NBA. For some reason, they left Sean out. Sean's disability is downs-syndrome and he is incredibly bright and outgoing. Sean sat Crying and wailing, it's not fair! IT's just not fair!

Grannie hog ma with compassion, questioned SEAN, What's up Seanny Sean!? Snort, Snort. What the smell? Why are you crying?

SEAN, immersed with tears of sadness exclaimed, they won't let me play Grannie Hog Ma! Why am I treated so badly? They don't realize how gifted and talented I am!

Grannie Hog Ma remarks, you are right and we will see about that! (She rips off her break away dress and break away rubber boots.) I don't go anywhere without my B-Ball outfit and Red Chuck Taylors! Let's go and play little fella. We will show these chumps! By the way Sean, HERE comes your fifteen minutes of fame what position DO YOU PLAY?

He looks over at Grannie Hog Ma with a proud grin and says, REFEREE, now Grannie I must make the call, sorry, but you travelled!

Grannie say's snort, snort, what the smell!

Song: "Now Gimmee THAT BALL!" written by T. Cobb Morgan

Now Gimme THAT BALL, alright now we're playing basketball!
Now Gimme THAT BALL, alright now we're playing basketball!

Now Gimme THAT BALL (5 xs's)
When you get the ball
Aim for the moon…Air Ball!
NOW TRY not to release too soon.
Stay in the Groove & very smooth…Alley oop!

Now Gimme THAT BALL, alright now we're playing basketball!
Now Gimme THAT BALL, alright now we're playing basketball!
Now GIMME THAT BALL (5 x's)

Jordan, Johnson, Byrd, West. All in their splendor,
Kareem Abdul Jabar…WASN'T HE Lew Alcindor?
Chuck Cooper, Earl Lloyd, WATARU MISAKA, Manuel Raga
(Who were they?)
THE FIRST, blacks, Asian and Mexican greats in the NBA!
RAISE YOUR arms in the air AND TURN AROUND REAL tall,
Now YOU'RE DOING IT, you're doing THE BASKETBALL!

Now Gimme THAT BALL (5 x's)
Ahru, AHRU, Ahru, AHRUALL,
That means GIMME MY BASKETBALL!
        T. COBB MORGAN: LizLL03@aol..com

STOP and Reflect! To Work on WJF Worksheet, Journal and FOCUS at the end of this chapter or CONTINUE.

Manifestation end of Chapter Sixteen
"NOW gimme that ball"
WJF – Gifts to Glorify god!

PRAYER: Pray for 26 seconds on Topic of Focus - Biblical Manifestation: Glorify God with your gifts

DEVOTION: TAKE 26 minutes to read I Corinthians 12:26-31

26 If one part suffers, every part suffers with it; if one part is honored, every part rejoices with it.
27 Now you are the body of Christ, and each one of you is a part of it. 28 And God has placed in the church first apostles, second prophets, third teachers, then miracles, then gifts of healing, of helping, of guidance, and of different kinds of tongues. 29 Are all apostles? Are all prophets? Are all teachers? Do all work miracles? 30 Do all have gifts of healing? Do all speak in TONGUES [d]? Do all interpret? 31 Now eagerly desire the greater gifts. I Corinthians 12:26-31

Journal: What do you consider your spiritual gifts? And, what are your natural talents?

Fish Quote:

> Were you blessed with gifts spiritually? Or perhaps you were blessed with talents, quite naturally. Just make sure you glorify the givers from the Trinity!
> T. COBB MORGAN

Journal Entry

17

FORGIVE AND FORGET
WJF – Kneel and Keep Praying

River is holding cooler with Pink lady inside)
Pink Lady wake up, you're home.

PINK LADY moans, Take me to the water River.

SHE Slowly DUNKS AND BATHES THEN HUMS AND SINGS one verse of "takes me to the water".

River looking out over the river, how could they do those evil things to me? All the lies, deceit, cheating and mind games were so cruel. I thought I knew those two people so well. Now I feel as though I didn't know them at all.

Pink Lady empathizes, River, I have three priceless pieces of advice for you. First, clear your head, heart and soul. Secondly, remove yourself from the situation. Thirdly, think on forgiveness. Your head says, "I'm not so sure I will forgive right now." Your heart says, "Maybe I will forgive." The soul says I must forgive to live."

YOU are right Pink Lady. I must forgive and move on. Thanks for the spiritual advice, the song and being my confidant- Girl, take a bow. Bravo! (Claps his hands) ... Goodnight.

Goodnight, River.

JOURNAL ENTRY:

STOP and Reflect! To Work on WJF Worksheet, Journal and FOCUS at the end of this chapter or CONTINUE.

Manifestation end of Chapter Seventeen
"FORGIVE AND FORGET"
WJF – Kneel and keep praying for everything!

PRAYER: Pray for 26 seconds on Topic of Focus - Biblical Manifestation: kneel and keep praying for everything!

DEVOTION: TAKE 26 minutes to read chapter and challenge question.

Study Bible
Jesus Prays at Gethsemane
...38Then He said to them, "My soul is consumed with sorrow to the point of death. Stay here and keep watch with me." 39Going a little farther, He fell facedown and prayed, "My Father, if it is possible, let this cup pass from Me. Yet not as I will, but as You will." 40Then Jesus returned to the disciples and found them sleeping. "Were you not able to keep watch with me for one hour?" He asked Peter.... Matthew 26:38-40

JOURNALIZE: Journalize each day.
Where was Jesus during his prayer?
What position did He pray IN?
Who accompanied Jesus?

Lord, Must I Kneel During Prayer in My Wheelchair?

Lord, I thank you that I can rest in my bed as I pray for spine strength, to sit up in my chair,

People, if you have strong legs and a spine then wave praise to HIM in the air,

Lord, I would honor you on my knees if they weren't so painful from wear and tear,

Lord, I thank you for the power to stand as I pray to get out this wheelchair,

Lord, I thank you for the ENDURANCE TO run the RACE AS I PRAY FOR the sun on my face and the wind in my hair,

I thank you for your awesome favor and trust that you will always be there!

God said, Beloved, don't worry about your condition, just keep believing me and hearing from me I love you in my care,

I I'm just happy you still meet with me with fresh flowers of praises for me in your SWEET HOUR OF PRAYER.

T. Cobb Morgan

18

THE CHRONICLES OF RIVER
WJF – I will Make You Fishers of Men

MAN, I DIDN'T get much sleep last night and what I had, was choppy and restless complained a tired River. Where did the crazy nightmares come from? Speaking to himself, pencil tapping on the desk while holding for Loretta, his favorite Human Resources Manager, always makes her calls worth the wait. She picks up the telephone.

Hello Loretta. This is River. How are you doing today? I really need your Human Resources expertise. Yes, here's the scenario, I have three part-time displaced Special Needs employees because of our recent layoffs. Although they have been proactive in seeking employment, they have been unsuccessful in their attempts.

River, you must be living right, I am delighted to help you in any way possible. By the way, I was so sorry to hear about your broken engagement. Shame to your fiancé, she will regret her decision. Aside, from my husband, you're the total package!

Yeah, total package huh? Then why is it when we are marked C.O.D (Cash on Delivery), you women send our brown boxed packages back return mail! They laugh.

River you're something else. I've great news for you I just reviewed three positions for post. They are mail room ready but the applicants must be able to operate a scanner, maintain confidentiality and lift ten-pound mail bundles. Keep in mind they are part-time and unfortunately no benefits. However, depending on next year's budget, we may be able to remedy that.

Excellent! Thanks, so much Loretta. When will the positions become available? Great, will do. Listen, lunch on me girl. Oh no, I will bring it to your office. Yes, I met your husband, Taylor aka "Big Swoll" at the Christmas party and I am not trying to bench press that big guy on my lunch hour. They laugh. Ok, thanks again, see you next Monday. HANGS UP PHONE

River approaches Kween Amaya's desk and greets her. Good morning Kween Amaya, how is my college bound cousin doing on her internship? And, is Don free for a minute?

"Top of the morning to you," smiles Amaya in her Native Jamaican accent. A million island sunrises to you cousin River for helping me with this position. I love it and Clara in the Legal Department promised me an opportunity to review some Shipbuilding cases. Hold on, she presses the call button on her phone, "Mr. Mills Line One."

Her smile retreats and her eye drops, I was so sorry to hear about your engagement being broken. Kween quickly recants, you know that woman was beneath you and your best friend didn't deserve your friendship. Say the word River and I will a cast a "side eye" spell upon the crooked couple. Also, I have a seven-day chicken feet and oxtail potion just for what ails you River!

Whoa, as tempted as I am Kween Amaya, I must refrain. If it gets to be too much I'll let the air out of their tires.

Don walks by him looking disheveled with coffee, sorry about the wait River, but no more bad news today, please. Oh by the way, sorry to hear about your engagement.

What? You know too? I've got to find myself some new friends and a bigger town. I have good news. With the assistance of Loretta Taylor in Human Resources we able could offer the special needs team part-time positions with weekends off. I am especially proud that they volunteered to enroll in the six-week company workshops offering three credit hours towards an associate degree.

Don commends him, great job River.

Thanks Don. So, what was the bad news you received today?

Come Closer River, this is top secret information. We, the naval yard contractors, are being forced to pay the Feds an extravagant illegal dumping fee beginning next year. I've been working with an FBI agent to get to the bottom of this situation. I believe they are using me to extract information regarding any illegal activity on the docks.

River scratching his head replies, Don this sounds serious. Let me ask you something. Do you have a plan? Are you wearing a wire? Do you carry a weapon? Do you have a contact person/inside spy? If the answers to those questions reflect the times you have said no to those doughnuts over there in the pretty pink boxes, then you need some help.

That's it River! You need to find US a pretty pink box, in other words, a distraction, to get us in the door of the organization. I'm really impressed with your security experience and business acumen. If we work together we can strangle the life out of this crude operation that is polluting our waterways and citizens drinking water. Not to mention a few crooks on city council.

River, concerned, Wait a minute. What do you mean "we?" He looks around, sorry no French speaking guy over here!

Oh, I think you'll learn the language when you review my offer. First, let's renegotiate your work contract to Senior Officer with a 20% raise matched by a 20% end of the year bonus. I'll throw in a $20,000 corporate card and upgrade your company car.

River, mimics, Oui, Oui Monsieur!

Don, great! Let's discuss the details after my 2:00 p.m. Meeting. Go get them River!

River, sounds like a plan to me.

Sounds like a plan to me.

Pond shouts, what are you doing?!

Lake to Pond, hey dude, get READY; we are in for a mission.

Pond to lake…yeah, YEAH, mission imps sib

FADE OUT

FADE IN

INT EILEEN'S FLOWER SHOP-AFTERNOON

River calls Eileen at the flower shop, "Hello Ms. Eileen."

Eileen welcomes River. Hello Mr. River. I was so sorry to hear about your broken engagement. Your ex-fiancée called in to apprise me that you two amicably broke off the engagement and would not need the flowers.

May I please have a copy of the Chronicles of River? It seems I was the only one who didn't receive a copy. By the way, here are the bouquet samples I am returning. You did a beautiful job on these. Eileen, at the risk of being too forward, may I invite you to have lunch with me? Please oblige me. We can go to any restaurant of your choosing.

She chuckles. Now you've put me at the risk of sounding too accommodating. What's a girl to do and say?

He responds, a girl is to come have lunch with me and say yes.

Okay, yes.

FADE OUT

FADE IN

INT. SEAFOOD RESTAURANT - NOON

Eileen smiles, River, I'm stuffed. The grilled lemon chicken and blackberry cheesecake was outstanding. I was pleasantly surprised and impressed as you ordered an "Eileen" wine spritzer in my name! Ooh, those cheese biscuits just melted in my mouth. Thank you so much. The meal was first class and the service was five stars. This was a splendid dining experience.

River replies, Eileen are you serious? This is Red Lobster.

Why yes and I enjoyed it. I'm a foodie. If I have good food, good service and good company then we are good. I can't imagine why she let such a good catch swim away. If you don't mind what was your ex like?

Well Not nearly as refreshing as you for sure. I truly enjoy this restaurant but she wouldn't step foot in this place. She prided herself in being a size two and counted every calorie in hopes of landing a full-time modeling gig. She is a big dreamer but wanted me to make those dreams come. But she needs some polish on smiling and being kind to others. I suspect when she found out about Lark's $250,000 Big Rig truck settlement, she thumbed him down and hitch hiked a ride!

Eileen jumps in, or stowed away in the back!

Either way, I suspect she made her way to the front rig to ride shotgun. I wish them well.

Eileen, speaking of riding shotgun, I must get back to work to deliver a large flower order for a Wild, Wild West ranch Wedding party in Virginia Beach.

I'll take a shortcut. I wouldn't want you to miss the anticipated "Rooting Tooting good time!

I agree. I have a meeting with my boss. excuse me, waiter, may I have the check please. he pays cash and they leave.

Larkson and Delilah are in the back hiding behind their menus and lowers them to see River and Eileen leave.

Larkson motions Delilah, let's follow them and switch the briefcases.

DELILAH thinks to herself, I see it didn't take long for River to move on.

STOP and Reflect! To Work on WJF Worksheet, Journal and FOCUS at the end of this chapter or CONTINUE.

Manifestation end of Chapter Eighteen
"THE Chronicles OF RIVER"
WJF – I will make you fishers of men!

<u>PRAYER</u>: Pray for 26 seconds on Topic of Focus - Biblical Manifestation:
I – I will make you fishers of men

<u>DEVOTION</u>: Take 26 minutes to read chapter and challenge question.
Bible verses related to Fishers Of Men from the King James Version (KJV)
Who said the following VERSE?

<u>Matthew 4:19</u> - And he saith unto them, follow me, and I will make you fishers of men.
Who was Jesus talking to?

<u>Matthew 28:19</u> - Go ye therefore, and teach all nations, baptizing them in the name of the Father, and of the Son, and of the Holy Ghost:

JOURNALIZE: Take 26 hours (1 day + 2 hours) to journalize each day.

A FUN PROJECT for YOU AND THE KIDS!
Project: Upon reading the "Fishers of Men "verses above and the "Plan of Salivation below, draw a fish outline and paste, tape or staple the verses on either side of the fish cut-out.

"Plan of Salvation: John 5:24 - Verily, verily, I say unto you, He that heareth my word, and believeth on him that sent me, hath everlasting life, and shall not come into condemnation; but is passed from death unto life.

FISH QUOTE:

TEACH A CHILD to be fishers of men,
Then you have taught a home,
TEACH A home to be fishers of men,
Then you have taught a community,
TEACH a Community to be fishers of men,
Then you have changed the world.

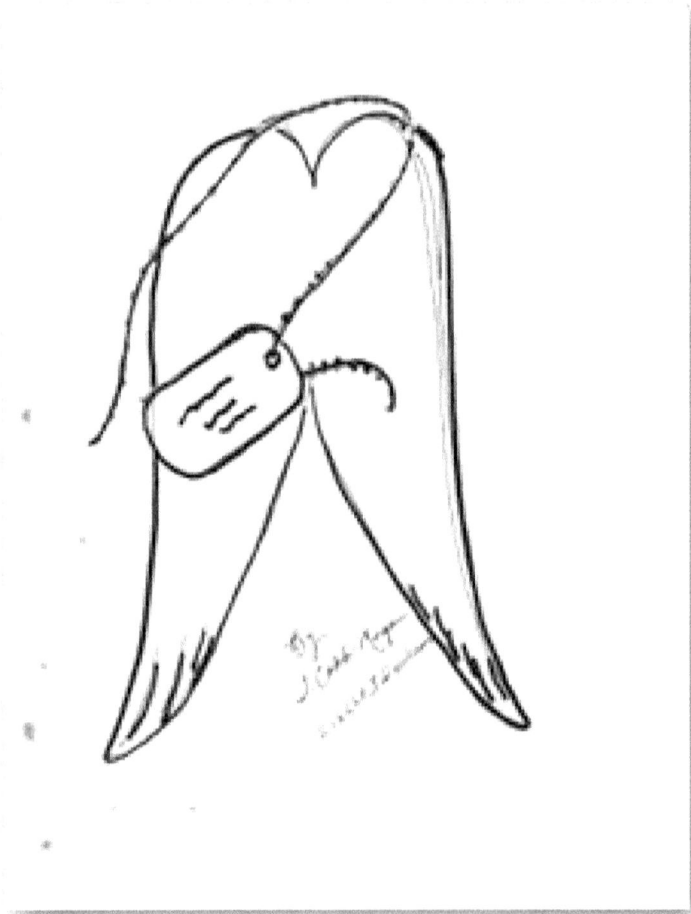

19

FALLEN SOLDIER AND RISEN ANGEL
WJF – Suffer to Glorify God

THE SUN IS setting and the day seemed long for River and he just wanted to relax with Eileen; but first, as with most mama boys he had to call his mother. River picks up his cell to check on her. Hi Mom, how are you? I just left work and I am exhausted. I called to see if you needed anything or some assistance before I head home. Is Dad with you? Wonderful Thanks, Mom, I Love you more.

He hangs up the phone. He notices Eileen's earring on the passenger seat. He calls Eileen.

Hello. May I speak to Eileen? Hi, what's going on Girl? I found your earring you "planted" on my passenger's seat. But the only female who will ride in my work van is Lady Gaga, my Auntie's cat! But my road dawg is Bear. THEY LAUGH. Eileen giggles, River, you're so funny! Girl, you are something else. So how was your day and were you able to get your large order out? Good job. You want me to drop off your earring? What is your address? One Land O'Lakes Court. Your condo color is Bisque colored wood and brick trim on corner lot. Cool. See you in ten minutes.

River whistles as he rings the door bell and hears a dog barking. The Virginia night air is crisp and cool. The trees swaying softly as the gentle breezes shimmers the leaves variations of color. Suddenly there's a playful knock at the door. Good evening River, Come on in. Besides my "daughter" niece Michelle this is my other child, my pug Denzel. He continues barking.

River comments, your daughter wants to shoot me and your son wants to bite me! They laugh and her pug retreats to his doggy bad. Would you like a glass of white wine? She twists her robe's sash and checks the turban tied towel of wet hair.

A presumptuous, but much appreciated, tall, ice chilled chardonnay wine goblet awaits him and she hands him the glass. Thank-you pretty lady, as he anxiously sips the wine trying not to gulp it down like a beer while his lips search for the head of suds. It is evident that there seems to be one wine connoisseur in the room and it ain't him. He is impressed with her periodic Italian Baroque theme condo splashed with elegant colors of African bronze, deep wine and silvery patina. His eyes scan the tastefully decorated room flanked by an alcove between two pillars showcasing a Bird of Paradise floral arrangement. Great condo Eileen, you're so on point with the Italian décor I'm waiting for Barry white and Luciano Pavarotti to jump out of the closet to sing "You're my first, my last my everything" hand me a plate of spaghetti a bottle of chardonnay. I see florist owners do well. By the way, here is your earring.

She thanks him as she happily puts on her earring, thinking out loud, how could I be so careless? Bear could have swallowed my 18kt. Egyptian earring. She put on the unique deeply colored gold earring.

Suddenly, his smile turned serious as he tried not to study the side of her face. "Wait a minute, how did she get that deep tissue burn on her face and was it a result of domestic violence from a previous relationship, an accident or abuse? River asked himself."

Her mental telepathy kicked in as SHE QUICKLY clarified, "River, It's from Iraq 2000." Trying not to appear distracted from the burn he begged her pardon.

River, it's alright, as she led him out of his awkwardness. She went on to comment how others pretend not to notice the burn on the side of her face. I normally cover it with make-up when I go out. On occasion when I'm in need of adoration I call it my Purple Heart sensation in recognition of my girlfriend's high uniform decoration.

Looking confused, he commented, "girlfriend? Where is she? Are you...

...No, I'm not gay. However, I don't judge people by whom they belong and love. I wish my situation was that simple. River digs further, "May I ask what happened? That is, only if you feel comfortable talking to me about it.

Well, River, to be honest with you, I'm still healing physically, mentally, emotionally and I thank God every day...spiritually. Although it has been years since the incident, it feels like it happened yesterday. Our Medic chopper was revving up to head back to camp. I had just finished breakfast. My girlfriend, Kat was with me.

We were happily preparing to leave Iraq that morning in 2000. Kat asks me, "Eileen, do you have everything?

I told her yes, and then quickly remembered left my makeup bag with our friendship necklaces inside the tent.

Eileen, you would forget your name if it wasn't tattooed on your neck! (they laugh.) I will never forget her laugh. We have been laughing since second grade. The first day of school I was so frightened I started to cry. Kat came over to me and said, "What's your name? I was embarrassed because my front teeth were missing. I covered my mouth with my hand and whispered, "Eileen."

"Well Eileen only sissies cry. My name is Katrina and if we are going to be friends you'd better toughen up. In fact, my new nickname for you is "Scrap Iron." I'm not a bully but I can bring the heat when needed."

From that day on Kat and I were inseparable, friends, no we were "SISTERS" for life. Even when we joined the army together, her husband Michael was there at the ceremony with their four-year old daughter Michelle.

As the bus pulled away Michelle started crying, Mommy come back! I want to be a soldier nurse with you! Mommy, please come back to my heart! That was the first time I ever saw Katrina cry.

Kat told me, Eileen, it breaks my heart to leave my baby. I'll do my committed four years in Army Medic and earn my nursing degree. After that I am going back home to be a trauma nurse in Virginia. When you have your children, I will always give them free medical care. So far, I only have Daisy, your Pomeranian to work on! Do you still want to be a florist?

Damn right, I'll have the best shop in Virginia. I'll send you fresh flowers on your birthday. Every year I get to remind you that you're older than me.

Kat closes her eyes and remembers her honeymoon with Michael in Hawaii. She and Eileen were lucky enough to have their graduations there. Their special guests were Michael and two-year old Michelle. Ooooh, I can smell them now, the Maui bouquet with Island Orchids and Birds of Paradise! You gave it to me for my wedding bouquet.

River queries, "Where is she now?"

Eileen pauses, I'm getting there, allow me to continue. The Iraqi morning began so nice. After getting fresh air we were headed for a last check.

Kat asked, Eileen, you secure the remaining medical supplies and I'll go back for the make-up bag.

Eileen responds, Too Easy! I walked back to the tent, my smile quickly turned upside down into a frown as I looked up at the dark Smokey Iraqi sky. The clouds were smothering the sun as it dimmed to a coppery color. Then out from nowhere, hostile fire ascended upon our camp. Grenades! I ran into the tent and yelled Katrina! The tent is full of smoke! We must go...where are you? She coughed, "Eileen."

I gasped as I turned around to find her in a fetal position with fifty percent of her body suffering third degree burns. I will never forget her horrific image or the smell of her flesh burning. The walk back was too far for her. I pulled out my knife and slashed a cross through the tent. I yelled "In the name of Jesus, help someone, please!"

He appeared like the Angel Gabriel. I thought he was Gabriel!

Who did you think was Gabriel, asked River?

She replied, the tall handsome male soldier who stepped through the cross and carefully wrapped her in a blanket and lifted her into his arms. I passed out from smoke and shock. When I came to, Katrina and I were on a Medic helicopter headed for a burn unit hospital in Germany. She was wrenching in pain from the fire and awful burns to her skin. She prayed in and out of consciousness asking God to bring her family to her. We were both faith-based believers and I held her as the medic treated her burns. She will need skin grafts, he said. I will be a skin donor and whatever else she needs; just save her I beg you! Kat held on long enough for Michael and Michelle to get there to say good-bye. She died in his arms as Michelle slept beside her.

RIVER sniffled and said, "I'm so sorry."

Eileen continued, on her birthday, July 14th, Michelle and I put a fresh Maui Bouquet on her grave. As I reach down to put the flowers on her grave, flashbacks of his arm still haunt me to this day.

RIVER replied, "Whose arm?"

I am talking about the arm of the soldier who saved us. As he reached for us and later closed our chopper door, I vividly remember a pair of wings tattooed on his forearm that read…

RIVER holds out his arm and reads,

…Sarah's wings.

EILEEN cries, OH my God, River, how did you know that? (She pauses) It's you! She walks over and pushes up his shirt sleeve. When she sees the inscription "Sarah's Wings" they look at each other and passionately kiss.

River, a faith-based believer holds her all night and prays for her on the sofa. At 5:00a.m. Michelle was going to get gas and Denzel had to pass gas. He accommodated them both, saw Michelle off to D.C., put Denzel back in the house and Eileen's keys on the table He thanked God because he found his future wife, daughter and son.

RIVER SINGS SONG, "THERE'S NO DISABILITY IN HER SWEET ENGAGING SMILE".

STOP and Reflect! To Work on WJF Worksheet, Journal and FOCUS at the end of this chapter or CONTINUE.

Manifestation end of Chapter nineteen
Fallen Soldier and risen Angel'
WJF - Suffer to glorify god

PRAYER: Pray for 26 seconds on Topic of Focus - Biblical Manifestation: S- Suffer to glorify God

DEVOTION: Take 26 minutes to read chapter and challenge question. S- SUFFER To glorify God

I Corinthians 12:21 -27
[21] The eye cannot say to the hand, "I don't need you!" And the head cannot say to the feet, "I don't need you!" [22] On the contrary, those parts of the body that seem to be weaker are indispensable, [23] and the parts that we think are less honorable we treat with special honor. And the parts that are unpresentable are treated with special modesty, [24] while our presentable parts need no special treatment. But God has put the body together, giving greater honor to the parts that lacked it, [25] so that there should be no division in the body, but that its parts should have equal concern for each other. [26] If one part suffers, every part suffers with it; if one part is honored, every part rejoices with it.
[27] Now you are the body of Christ, and each one of you is a part of it.
I Corinthians 12:21-27

JOURNALIZE:

1Therefore, since we have been justified through faith, we have peace with God through our Lord Jesus Christ, **2**through whom we have gained access by faith into this grace in which we now stand. And we[b] boast in the hope of the glory of God. **3**Not only so, but we also glory in our sufferings, because we know that suffering produces perseverance; **4**perseverance, character; and character, hope. **5**And hope does not put us to shame, because God's love has been poured out into our hearts through the Holy Spirit, who has been given to us

FISH QUOTES:

Quitters will never experience hope because they lack the integrity to persevere.
T. Cobb Morgan

I was so "wowed by heaven where everything looked polished and new.
Until an angel said you're not in heaven, this

Is the passage through to see if your life has been true?
(River's Heavenly Encounter)

PART 3

20

MISSION IMPOSSIBLE
WJF – X Marks the Spot to a More Successful You

THE EARLY MORNING fishing pier is eerily calm and River is anxiously looking for Pink Lady Sassy Bass. The Virginia weather is ideal kindly displaying a cool temperature of 70 degrees.

Pink Lady! Pink Lady! shouts, River.

Pink lady slowly emerges and yawns a "Good morning River. I hope your formulated plan works because I don't do 5:30 a.m. well"!

RIVER assures her, "Relax Pink Lady. Everything will work out fine. Now let's review the fine tuned plan which reads like a script! Precisely at 6:30 a.m., we will roll out "Operation Stinky River" to see who is behind the illegal waste dumping and polluting the river."

Pink Lady interrupts, River, will I have adequate security? This sounds like risky business!

RIVER, reassures her, "I'm one step ahead of you. Bubba's Bad Bass will escort you out of Freshwater Fish Farm in a seaweed covered crab basket coach. They will exchange you for the briefcase at the drop off point, Saltwater River Mills. Tony's Treacherous Thug fish will surround your excursion to the Riverbanks Country Club by 8:00 a.m."

PINK LADY ponders, "Wait a minute, and DOESN'T Tiny weigh 300 pounds?"

RIVER nervously responds with a quick, "Oh yeah, and don't forget his razor-sharp K-9 teeth. So, if he wants to be called Tiny, we will call him Tiny!" His toothy sinister smile wouldn't exactly land him a wholesome peanut butter commercial."

PINK LADY responds, good observation. Now explain to me again, how do I keep getting caught up in your crazy life? River, this is a dangerous mission, thuggish, top secret operations, this sounds like something in the sea movies. Water wood, here I come! Watch out Halibut Berry and Angela Bass. River, proceed with your plan until I am convinced!

RIVER continues, "Upon shore, the Wayward Walking Catfish will further escort your incognito coach to the edge. My boss, Don will be having a breakfast meeting with the crooked members' crew. I'll be dressed as a waiter with a silver covered tray. Once the meeting is complete, I will handoff the recording device to you with the illegal procedures. Secure it and head back home to Freshwater farms. Pink Lady, I'm counting on you, but if at any time, you feel the least bit threatened or compromised, then activate your body wire switch and abort the operation."

PINK LADY, changes her mind and remarks, "No way. This mission is resume 'and portfolio worthy! Upon my return, I will call the newspaper, Ocean Times and get on the phone to Shonda Scandal Fish Rhymes, Osprey Win free publicity, Tycoon Perry and Dancing Seal Ellen! Pink Lady appeals to River's inner child, Pond. Considering his eyes, "Shouldn't you have a River Doo speed boat or something to rescue me as we escape up the river James Pond style?"

POND is impressed and chimes, yes that sounds so cool! Lake is imagining himself as James Bond driving a speedboat to James Bond music.

RIVER, answers, sorry, it's not in the budget. PINK LADY differs, "Mm mph that's what you think. This is my big break."

RIVER double checks his equipment, "Now test your waterproof phone so we can secure contact. THEY TEST. Great! Work your magic Pink Lady and please be careful. I will meet you back here at 12:00 noon."

PINK LADY waves her fin, Toddles, be careful River.

"Sure thing" answers River. He heads for the COUNTRY CLUB PATIO in search of Don, River's boss. Don is meeting with the businessmen of The Pinnacle Company over breakfast to discuss their waste dumping needs and proper measures to accept bids for waste preparation, sterilization and drain.

Don turns to River and winks, "Excuse me young man. My E, eggs Benedict entree' is not up to par. Please bring me a lighter fare; perhaps, a vegetable omelet? Oh, and pour me another champagne please." River obliges, "Yes sir."

Business Member One is anxious to get down to business. So, Don, did you bring the contract agreeing to underbid the Gross Waste Dumping Company. We have been their major client for years.

Don tries to cover his annoyance with the Business Member Crook. Why, yes of course. But you do realize we at ACME Waste add an antibacterial solvent that doubles as a detergent to cleanse the river water. However, we clear any restrictions with the government first.

The second (2nd) Business member two scoffs at the feds practices and comments, pesky feds, they always manage to tie up legal matters with their bright red tape!

Don's for a confession, "Your previous company doesn't ensure safety measures in place. Furthermore, they do not advise the government nor do they add a solvent to control the bacteria. Were you aware of these injustices?"

Business members both face each other, we just order the sausage. We don't care about how it's made! They laugh.

Don, shakes his head in agreement, I see. Gentlemen, please print, date and sign your names on the highlighted areas. The Business Member Crooks both pull out matching pens. Don suspects they are using invisible ink and insist they use his pen for signature uniformity. Although hesitant, the gentlemen sign. Now gentlemen I will get you a copy and he snaps his finger at River. "excuse me again young man would you get me a copy of this contract? And where is your restroom?

River guides him and says, "Right this way Sir." They exit patio and rush through main lobby to exit front door. A limo awaits don.

Don, although obviously shaken; maintains his composure and fumbles to get his glasses on. As he positions behind the limo He looks up at River and says, "River, I will forever be indebted to you, thanks for a spectacular plan, good job River!

River reminds Don, "We are not out of the woods yet." He grabs a briefcase off the table. Stay on plan and make sure my mother gets this briefcase. Limo drives off.

Security team is watching via the security cam in the upstairs balcony. Larkson Nedo, with binoculars in hand is watching too…

Larkson Nedo commands, the security Team. Security! There he is! Quick get him! (Goons one and two charge him)

River Jerks his neck from side to side, cracks his knuckles and prepares for a fight. He tosses around furniture. Hey, come this way you two goons. Take this! (kick-boxes goon one).and you take that! (he elbows goon two and he doubles over his stomach causing him great pain.)

Larkson Nedo reinforces his command, "you idiots call yourselves security? Take him down now!" (goons three and four charge him.)

River (grunts and hits goon three with left hook and right leg kick box knocking him out! Other goon four jumps on river's back. River swings around and throws him over his shoulder on. River runs into another area and manages to hide in a large broom closet.

Goons four and five taunts river to appear and they, playfully mimic, "come out, come out wherever you are...or you're a dead man!

River, whispers to himself, what is this? Hide and go seek? He hides behind the hotel president's wife's portrait. He quickly punches out the canvass outlining her face and replaces it with his and drapes a tablecloth around him.

Goon five, passes by River. River's face is protruding as he wears the portrait. The goon remarks, Oh my god, what a Big Ugly Broad! He continues walking about ten steps. Wait a minute... turns around and lunges toward River.) Wait a minute, who do you think you're fooling?

RIVER, (Sarcastically) I certainly cannot pull the wool over your eyes. Tag, you're it! He slams a portrait over goon five's head and runs toward side door. River runs into the waiter with a full ice bucket and carafe of water causing it to spill. Goon Six slips and falls. River runs around side of country club and dives into the river to escape. Pink lady, where are you?

Pink lady pops up. River, over here! Quick! (she loosened a speed boat's rope for river to escape. River jumps off pier in slow motion.

Hurry, no time to talk they are gaining on us! Start the boat! The motor hesitates. River yells, Pink Lady it won't start!

Pink lady looks around in desperation and says, you who, oh Tiny!

TINY "JAWS" THUGFISH gets into position, don't worry Pink Lady we got you. I'll do my Jaws Pose!

TINY JUMPS UP ON PIER WITH HEAD UP EXPOSING SHARK BODY FULL K-9 FANGS.

RAAAWWWWW! GROWL!

"SECURITY TEAM" backs are out running the club patrons! Whoa! Oh, my God, it's Jaws! Run! They and the dining guests run full speed.

River's MOTOR STARTS. Here we go Pink Lady! (THEY SPEED OFF DOWN THE RIVER and the chasing boat U turns and heads back to the country club. River thinks they home free as he waves to his boss on the river bank. (Stands and Yells) Hey Don, we did it!

(the boat hits a rock and the Boat turns upside down into a full explosion. River is blown 20 feet to an island like patch of dirt and a boulder rock is exposed. He is knocked out and has a head injury as he falls onto the ground.

Pink Lady

River! Are you okay? Oh no, he is not breathing! (She notices an extremely bright, almost blinding glimmer between the boulders split beside his HEAD). Oh no, he is seeing the light! River, come away from the light! (She sends out a sonic message to the fish to swim to her) Quick! Tiny and Thug fish please swim under him and take him to shore. Grandma Sarah? Are you out there? Please send River a wakeup call! Please! Blowfish keep blowing oxygen into him. Stingray and Blue crab sting and pinch him to wake-up his SENSES, on the count of three 1-2-3!

FADE OUT

FADE IN

INT – HOSPITAL ROOM WITH RIVER - AFTERNOON

Liz is leaning over him) River, baby if you can hear me please squeeze my finger on the count of three.

Grannie Hog Ma

(Coming out of bathroom spraying can of Gardenia freshener, hair disheveled, skirt pulled up to breast)

Snort, Snort, what the smell? Lord, Child that Collard green, egg nog prune breakfast diet shake is churning and burning my stomach! Oh, no I feel as though I'm Farting a symphony of flatulence. Oh, my goodness, bronk, bronk, there goes the tuba section! I can't control these bootie burps! I got to go home and sit on my own throne while fanning her bootie. Liz I'll check on River later. In the meantime, I might have to change my bloomers!

River has been in a coma for three days and he's dreaming about a song his mother wrote, "THE TREE of life."

Song: Tree of Life
Written by Terry Morgan, LizLL03@aol.com

I'm not here to rock the mic, throw it up to the universe and
make it spike,
I'm here out of sheer delight to tell you about my story of Tree of Life.
God said it, He meant it, get with it, Be ready!
One day I was riding down the river's bed and fell in and hit my
head
I even heard someone said he has got to be dead,

They were praying for a miracle because I just bled…and
bled ….and bled.
I thought it was all over until I saw this bright light, I was drawn into
this miraculous sight it almost blinded me with fright! When it swallowed the night!
I had never seen anything like this before – a land of miracles, wonders
and signs galore! God said it, He meant it, get with it, Be Ready!
I saw the little girl with palsy come out of her rest, and the woman
who touched the hem of his garment out of desperation indication of
a healing creation that still stuns nations with sensations of faith and
scientific" communications
I was so "wowed by heaven where everything looked polished and new.
Until an angel said you're not in heaven, this
Is the passage through to see if your life has been true? As she turned
around it was evident her vision of loveliness and words quite clever,
This Goddess was fine right out of the book Songs
of Solomon endeavor.
Beauty by Queen Esther, Body by Bathsheba, Wisdom by Judge Deborah!
Faith by Hannah, Courage by Mary, Businesswoman by Lydia,
what style,

Her sultry walk by Cleopatra, that's got to be Gorgeous Delilah's smile!
As I reached for her arm, Caesar & Marc Anthony chased me with a
knife,
She got back on her boat "The River Nile" she shouted hurry, River
run for your life!
Then the most beautiful angel, Grandma Sarah, stopped me in my tracks,
As much as I love you River you must go back!

She showed me a river of the water of life, clear as crystal,
a refreshing spring,
coming from the throne of God and of the Lamb, yes, our Savior the King,
In the middle of its street. On either side of the river was the Tree of life,
bearing twelve kinds of fruit, every month for our delight
God said it, He meant it, get with it, Be ready!
The leaves were for the healing of the nations.
Check it out in the book or wait for the revelation,
No curses abide the throne of God and the Lamb in it,
And His bond-servants will serve Him and get with it…

God said it, He meant it, get with it, and Be ready! …
God's purpose for you has not been fulfilled, so on the count of three…
Click your leather boots three times, tell all you meet about the King!!
FADE OUT
FADE IN

PINK LADY
PINK LADY- River, can you hear me? On the count of Three (3), I
want you to wake up! One,
One…
LIZ

MOM – Please son, you must come through on the count of Two
Two

SARAH-THE ANGEL
Grandma Sarah –Grandson, you can't come with
me, so wake up on Three
Three!

River? (His eyes open) Thank God, you're awake!

Mom I'm okay but just a little groggy. Why am I
here in the hospital? What's going ON? Mom, you
look tired.
River, Hush baby don't talk. You were in an accident.
Please try to rest. I've been here awhile and I must go
home to rest. I just need to take care of myself.
River says OK; but now, promises me you will get
some rest.

Eileen is here to see you. Get some rest we will
call you in the morning. I love you.
FADE OUT
FADE IN

STOP! To Work on WJF: Worksheet, Journal REFLECT & FOCUS at the end of each chapter or CONTINUE.

Manifestation end of Chapter Twenty
"Mission Impossible"
WJF - X Marks the spot to successful you!

<u>**PRAYER**</u>: Pray for 26 seconds on Topic of Focus - **Biblical Manifestation: X marks the spot to a more successful you!**

<u>**DEVOTION**</u>: TAKE 26 minutes to read chapter and challenge question.

2 Chronicles 26:1-5 New International Version (NIV)
Uzziah King of Judah
26 Then all the people of Judah took Uzziah,[a] who was sixteen years old, and made him king in place of his father Amaziah. [2] He was the one who rebuilt Elath and restored it to Judah after Amaziah rested with his ancestors.
[3] Uzziah was sixteen years old when he became king, and he reigned in Jerusalem fifty-two years. His mother's name was Jekoliah; she was from Jerusalem. [4] He did what was right in the eyes of the LORD, just as his father Amaziah had done. [5] He sought God during the days of Zechariah, who instructed him in the FEAR [b] of God. If he sought the LORD, God gave him success.

<u>**JOURNALIZE AND POLISH YOUR PURPOSE**</u>: When it comes to success in life sometimes we must fake it until we make it.

Can you recall an opportunity you proved to be a great success despite odds of failure?

FISH Quote:

Decide very carefully how much y0u want success and on what terms,
Will it be something you are proud of, worked hard FOR WITH no integrity burns?
Or will it be something you carelessly tossed around and you never earned,
Be thankful of the blessings you receive with success BECAUSE it's a teacher who will make you learn!

T. Morgan

Lizgirl58@gmail.com

21

LUNCH AND A MOVIE
WJF – Excuse Me I think You are Leaking!

THE BASS RESIDENCE is slowly showing signs of a serene and clean transformation. The smell of woodsy pine cleaner and zesty lemon fresh dust polish oil is bringing the once stale and dusty place back to a home. MG hired a part-time maid to keep everything in order. Besides, it would take him all day just to dust Liz's Knick knacks. MG, sighs, what a week Liz, Good Morning. You're up early. How are you feeling?

Liz clears her voice, Good morning. I'm fine considering all the excitement this week. River's Un-Engagement Party, Lark and Delilah's Confession and…Artie and Miriam's A/C Jewelry Heist!

They both laugh at the name Miriam?

Liz replies on a serious note, "I thank God for River's recovery from the boating accident."

MG agrees, "He's fine and our family remained calm and prayerful, especially our grandchildren. I am so proud of them."

Liz's face lights up. "They amaze me. They simply amaze me! I admire their love, their trust and their fear of nothing. I used to be like that. I miss that. Parkinson's stole it all from me."

MG tells her, "You gave it away. You don't have to miss out. Get back to living Liz. Let's go to the movie theatre and catch the ten a.m. Show this morning."

MG, Liz fumbles to find the words, "It's not that simple and too hard to explain. You don't understand what it's like to get up three hours early to go to an event. I get up at 5:30 a.m. aching and shuffling o to the toilet, mix fiber into a bottle of water and chase it with another, drench my muscles with alcohol, shower, pee every hour, eat, take all my supplements/ medication with twenty side effects. Then I smear on some make-up, carefully brush my shedding hair and get fully dressed. I'm tired, full of anxiety, pouring sweat and my inner child is playing with matches."

MG tries to understand and questions, "Isn't that menopause, dear?" They look at each other and exchange puzzling looks.

Liz gives in, "Give me a minute to grab my shawl."

Mg and Liz are up front at the movies. She is seated in her wheelchair at the end of the last row. Mg is seated beside her in a theatre chair. The movie is almost over and Liz is getting anxious about dodging the crowd and getting to the bathroom in time.

Liz starts squirming and nudges her husband, MG I must pee.

MG replies but is still looking at the movie screen, "Liz are you sure?"

After all, MG explains, "You just went at the beginning of the movie. Honey, this is the twist of the ending, can you hold it for a few more minutes? I'll rush you in before the movie credits."

Liz cries, "What am I…five?! I know when I should go potty MG.

MG, still looking the movie screen, "C'mon baby, but aren't you wearing one of those maximum pad thing-ees?

Liz fumes, "Yes, but I don't want to *deliberately* pee on myself! If I get wet it will feel like I have a pillow between my legs! Besides I don't want to run into anyone we know. My brain is only thinking about getting to the toilet or some convenient receptacle. The Parkinson's will cause my feet to stick to the floor and the water to start running."

MG finally looks away from the screen, "Okay, let's go. Thank God, there's one around the corner!"

As they get through the doors, Sister Maggie, their nosey informal Church Reporter, yells out "Wait up Sister Liz...is that you Deacon MG." Slow down, I have your goodies bag you left in the movie chair with leftover mustard flavored pretzels, two empty juice boxes, a depends and your hemorrhoid medication. Grannie Hog Ma told us in the Praying Pansies meeting that the pews were too hard for you Deacon.

"MG, flustered, exclaims, "Really Mom? Really? Geez, can't this wheelchair go any faster?

MG Hit the gas and don't turn around! If I stop to talk to her my fluids will start flowing. Please hurry!"

"Liz, do you realize we are speeding down a movie corridor!? And by the way, she's pretty fast to be on a cane." MG slows down a little and responds nearly out of breath, I think we lost her in a sea of elderly senior citizens. What are we doing Liz? Oh God, please don't send me to hell. My wife handed me the apple to speed up! Liz, you know Ms. Maggie is legally blind in one eye. Bless her heart.

Yes, well she can see pretty good out of the other one! Look, we will have to repent later. But for right now, turn here! Great we made it! She shuffles into stall.

MG is seated on bench behind huge potted plant) his pants are pulled way up. I see what Liz meant; I had to go to the restroom too.

Excuse me Sir. You dropped this. She hands him an ATM receipt wrapped around a ticket stub.

MG takes the receipt and thanks her.

No problem, I'm sure you would have done the same thing. She glances back at MG, "Hey aren't you the gentleman I met at the Peach Orchard?" In fact, I picked up your fruit receipt and placed it in your shirt pocket.

MG worries that Liz will recognize and question the Lady's intention and frankly, he does not care to give an explanation to a situation that is sheer coincidence. LADY, YOU'VE GOT TO STOP PICKING UP THINGS OFF THE GROUND. Please pardon me I'm looking for my wife. I'm married. And she's looking for me too. I 've got to go. Thanks again, have a nice day.

MOVIE PATRON, (Looking confused) Yes, you too.

A Man is panicking and has his two children. Somebody help! My son is choking! Please help!

MG quickly walks over to assess the situation. He asks the gentlemen, "What is his name and what did he swallow?"

Man replies, his name is Joshua and he swallowed a cherry pit! Please save him!"

MG instructs the man to call 911. "Joshua, I need you to cough real hard like a big boy. He's turning blue. MG whisks him up in a Heimlich maneuver, Joshua cough!"

THE CROWD ENCROACHES UPON THEM.

MG firmly advises the crow to move back. He shouts, "Everybody please move back! The child needs air!

Movie attendant clears the crowd and reassures, Emergency Medical coming through.

Joshua coughs and the pit blockage dislodges. the child speaks, Daddy, I'm thirsty and I want to go home.

MG rejoices, "Good boy! Well, my work here is done. Young men, the EMT's have the situation under control. I wish you well. Now I must leave to find my wife." They shake hands and he leaves. The crowd is clapping! For he's a jolly good fellow! Hooray!

The Child's Mother, Teal Ivy, walks up. "Oh, my God what is going on?! Josh! My baby!

Man answers his wife, "Babe, everything is fine. Thanks to that man behind you.

The Child's Mother, Teal Ivy, looks around and questions, "What man?

Man looks around, "He was just here a minute ago. I think he had a medical or fire security background because he did a smooth Heimlich maneuver on Joshua."

The Childs's Mother is disappointed, "I sure would like to thank him. What was he like?"

Man describes MG, "He is Late 50'or early 60's, nice looking with real thick moustache, starched jeans, one of those old-school players... he was a cool dude! Hey check this out. Here is a neatly pressed men's handkerchief he wiped Joshua's face with. It has a masonic symbol, the initial M and like expensive cologne."

The Child's Mother, Teal Ivy, vows, "I am signing us up for child safety classes when we get back home to Washington, D.C. Let's get the kids fed and head HOME. She pulls out the handkerchief and looks around. She shrugs, who are you, EM?

Liz, exhausted, struggles to get in her wheelchair.) Where were you?! I called and you didn't answer.

"Honey relax. I had to go to the bathroom too. My bladder is sixty years old! On the way, back a child was choking and I rendered some assistance until the ambulance arrived."

Liz answers, "Really, Is he alright? So, was that his mother who gave you her phone number? I saw her at the end of the hallway."

MG answers, "You must be kidding me. I never saw his mother. What woman? C'mon Liz. Really? I dropped my ATM receipt and ticket stubs. She was returning them to me. I was so distracted looking for you to relax in your chair."

"MG, are you interested in another woman?"

Yes Liz, that's what I need, an opportunity to disappoint another woman!

They both walk back to the car in silence.

FADE OUT

FADE IN

EXT. MOVIE PARKING LOT – AFTERNOON

INT. MG & LIZ SUV – AFTERNOON

MG looks at her and asks, Liz, what is really going on? Where is that adventurous flight attendant I dated? Where is my wife, the bank manager, who would run home on her lunch hour and whip up a pot of spaghetti in her heels? Where is my girl who possesses all the traits of the virtuous woman with confidence, sophistication and finesse? Can I get her back? May I please have my wife back?"

Liz, sniffles, MG, I don't know where she is. For several years now I've been shielding my face and struggling with this strange lost woman and the old Liz can't find her way back to me. I don't know what to do anymore. I'm broken, I'm feeling ugly and I'm leaking!

MG, So WWLD?

LIZ, perplexed says, what?

MG

WWLD…What Would Liz Do?

Liz answers, I don't know. I guess I would get a bottle of life's glue, toss the mirror and grab a mop! In fact, it's in Proverbs 31, "The Virtuous Woman."

THEY KISS.

MG smiles. That's my girl. He sings, "I've got sunshine on a cloudy day, when it's cold outside, I've got the month of May. I guess you say what can make me feel this way. My girl." Hey, you want to get in the back seat.

Liz retreats, "Sorry MG, I've got pee in my boots."

MG backs down and says, "Girl, you know how to kill the mood."

"Papi, we will see about that. When we get home, I'm going to light some strawberries and champagne candles, take a strawberries and champagne bath, put on my strawberries and champagne heels in bed since I can't wear them in the street and have some strawberries and champagne."

MG's interest heightens, "Oh you naughty Nana." (Distracted) Don't look now, but there is a Praying Pansy face pressed against your window.

Liz turns around slowly, oh my!

Sis. Maggy –Can I get ride, Deacon MG, wonderful deacon of the month?

MG- Sure.

Sis. Maggy— Whistles, C'mon Pansies! Deacon, you don't mind three more, do you? My bunions are killing me! Estelle got popcorn in her dentures, and had to hang them on your door knob to dry. Agatha, would you stop burping, don't bring no more homemade canned milk cheese and onion crackers! So, help me Gertrude if you don't roll down the window with your 5-10-year felon fish' frog and fritter farts, I'm going to put you out! Deacon and Mrs. Isn't it a lovely day?

Upon arriving home two hours later, the television is playing a sexy commercial. MG and Liz appear to be having a romantic moment. However, they are cuddled on *Processes of Cleansing:*

sofa snoring with all their clothes still on.

FADE OUT

STOP! To Work on WJF: Worksheet, Journal REFLECT & FOCUS at the end of each chapter or CONTINUE.

Manifestation end of Chapter Twenty-One
"LUNCH AND A MOVIE"
WJF- Excuse me, I think you are Leaking!

<u>PRAYER</u>: Pray for 26 seconds on Topic of Focus **- Biblical Manifestation: E – Excuse me, I think you're Leaking!**
What do you mean by "Leaking" in this text?
(Answer) Spiritual "Leaking<u>" is how the body, soul and spirit release waste and dangerous toxins that pollute each system.</u>
Question Two
The cleansing process for body is done with Answer: (<u>natural water H2O",)</u>

<u>**Question Three:**</u>
The soul involves "washing of the word – <u>The Holy Bible"</u>

Question Four: and for the spirit it is <u>Living water, The Holy Spirit.")</u>
However, I believe they all benefit if we pray out loud, think on good thoughts, meditate, read the Bible.

Body – Cleanse with Natural water.

Processes of Cleansing:
Spirit- Cleansed with Living Water. We are born with our spirit and it is made new/reborn again upon accepting Christ.
Soul- Your soul is cleansed by the washing of the word. Our souls are transformed by the renewing of our minds. Romans 12:2, "And be not conformed to this world: but be ye transformed by the renewing of your mind, that ye may prove what is that good, and acceptable, and perfect, will of God."

1 Peter 1:22-23, "Seeing ye have purified your souls in obeying the truth through the Spirit unto unfeigned love of the brethren, see that ye love one another with a pure heart fervently: Being born again, not of corruptible seed, but of incorruptible, by the word of God, which liveth and abideth forever."

Fish hook quote:

Natural water,

Living Water,

Washing of the Word,

God's PH level is the best man has ever heard.
Who will keep us sustained?
GOD Sends the Rain.
        T. Morgan

22

REWARDS FOR RIVER
WJF – Va Va Boom Sexy!

RIVER'S OFFICE – MORNING

(SIX MONTHS LATER

River arrives at his office and phones Eileen. She answers and River says, "Good morning Scrap Iron. Are you up? Is the shop open today? Well, put on a pot of your favorite "Java, Java Coffee Bean, Greatest Day I've Ever Seen." You're out? Come on Babe you've got to get going. Don't forget the bowling party tonight. You will be meeting my entire family. Don't be ridiculous, they will love you…because I love you. Gotta go, bye.

Don walks in and immediately tells River, "I'm really having a hard time honoring your request not to have a formal ceremony. The ACME Company alone is awarding you with a $5,000 reloadable credit card."

River says, Don that is great. My mother's Parkinson's charity will benefit greatly under A" Wheelchair Ramps for Kids, Granny and Papa

Rollin'Biz"! Disabled persons program. You would be surprised to know how many people are confined to their homes for months, even years, because of no ramp access.

River, your mother is amazing.

I must agree; indeed, she is. In getting back to the Operation River Clean Up project, there was a third party involved. She wishes to remain anonymous although she was very instrumental in the program's success. Her only request is to keep the river clean particularly for bass survival, implement procedures for limits on bass fishing and plant sweeter river wild grass to feed and hide infant bass. By the way, her P.S. "Do bring the Bass Masters Classics to Virginia. All anglers would pray for a perfect day on our waters."

His supervisor asks him who is this bass fish activist and why are they so interested in the bass survival? Wait a minute I read an anglers article that mentioned "All anglers pray for a perfect day on the water, especially when they are a contender in the Bass Master Classic. River do you know the board."

River comments sarcastically, oh yeah, over lunch, one of the classics was discussing his previous attempts for a win. Five bass totaling 29 pounds, 2 ounces won $300,000 along with the most coveted award in the sport of professional bass fishing. He does outstanding charity work too.

Don, thinks back as a child and remembers his summers in Virginia, especially swimming in the lake among the seemingly "sociable" Bass. Kidding around with River and says, if it is not him, then I'm beginning to wonder if "this person" is a Bass fish! They glob, glob around the Lake speaking fish! He laughs and River nervously chimes in.

RIVER (Voiceover) With the number of Bass family concerns and personal confessions I've made out here on the river, I thank God that big mouth bass don't talk... or do they?

Don insists River to take his offer. I still want to offer you a certificate and a trophy in your honor for such wonderful service you have given this company. Furthermore, you have recognition from the Mayor and Governor of this fine city and state. Please go over to Human Resources to make sure you have the required paperwork and I. D.'s to collect your bonuses.

River glances out the window and reminds Don of his fantastic view.

DON agrees and thanks him. He mentions that his two favorite sights of downtown are F-15 salutes during Veterans Day and the Christmas parade.

RIVER agrees and comments, (looking out the window) I can't believe that out there among the hustling and bustling, my soulmate is out there. The woman I will marry someday.

Well, River there is somebody for everybody. Continue to remain optimistic. Lady Fate will bring her to you…all in good time.

No Don she really is out there. She is a very nice woman.

DON doesn't quite know how to handle River's wishful thinking. "Poor fella", Don thought to himself. He just got dumped by his fiancée and duped by his best friend!

Sure, she is big guy. (He pats River on the back).

I'll see you later Don. She's waiting for me to go bowling later. See you on Monday.

Have a good weekend. Keep your chin up buddy. One day she will really be there and I will dance at your wedding!

RIVER smiles and says, "Will do." He runs out the car, and three women giggling from Human Resources yell out, "River you are so sexy!"

FADE OUT

STOP! To Work on WJF: Worksheet, Journal REFLECT & FOCUS at the end of each chapter or CONTINUE.

**Manifestation end of
Chapter Twenty-Two
"REWARDS for River"
WJF – VA VA Boom sexy!**

<u>**PRAYER**</u>: Pray for 26 seconds on Topic of Focus - **Biblical Manifestation: FAITH-BASED sexy**

<u>**DEVOTION**</u>: Take 26 minutes to read chapter and challenge on.

VA, VA Boom, FAITH-BASED SEXY! – Song of Solomon Chapter 1 (KJV). (Each group member read and explain)
¹ The Song of Songs, which is Solomon's.
² Let him kiss me with the kisses of his mouth: for thy love is better than wine
³ Because of the savor of thy good ointments thy name is as ointment poured forth, therefore do the virgins love thee. **Question One: What does this mean to you?**

⁴ Draw me, we will run after thee: the king hath brought me into his chambers: we will be glad and rejoice in thee, we will remember thy love more than wine: the upright love thee. **Question Two: How would you paraphrase this?**

⁵ I am black, but comely, O ye daughters of Jerusalem, as the tents of Kadar, as the curtains of Solomon.
⁶ Look not upon me, because I am black, because the sun hath looked upon me: my mother's children were angry with me; they made me

the keeper of the vineyards; but mine own vineyard have I not kept. **Question Three: In your opinion, why does she say this?**

[7] Tell me, O thou whom my soul loveth, where thou feedest, where thou makest thy flock to rest at noon: for why should I be as one that turneth aside by the flocks of thy companions?

[8] If thou know not, O thou fairest among women, go thy way forth by the footsteps of the flock, and feed thy kids beside the shepherds' tents.

[9] I have compared thee, O my love, to a company of horses in Pharaoh's chariots.

[10] Thy cheeks are comely with rows of jewels, thy neck with chains of gold.

[11] We will make thee borders of gold with studs of silver.

[12] While the king sitteth at his table, my spikenard sendeth forth the smell thereof.

[13] A bundle of myrrh is my well-beloved unto me; he shall lie all night betwixt my breasts.

[14] My beloved is unto me as a cluster of camphor in the vineyards of Engadin. **Question Four: Name three ways he compliments her?**

[15] Behold, thou art fair, my love; behold, thou art fair; thou hast doves' eyes.

[16] Behold, thou art fair, my beloved, and yea, pleasant: also, our bed is green.

[17] The beams of our house are cedar, and our rafters of fir.

Song of Solomon - <u>King James Version</u> (KJV)

IS Sexy NO LONGER SEXY? Today, it has new meaning. Anything can be sexy - a burger, car, song, book or even a cell phone. Watch out! Most of us want to "LOOK SEXY, ATTRACTIVE AND EXCITING" even if we won't admit it. Is it wrong for faith-based people to desire a physically attractive look? Not at all! God blessed us all with our unique gifts to draw others to Him (Our third purpose) Our body is God's temple to glorify Him and thank Him for being made in His image. Use your appeal to draw the masses to tell them about their "Trio Hero", your three-part self (Body, Soul and Spirit.) Your body's true sexiness should exude a caring heart, health in healing, empowering strength and daily maintenance of character if it is to reflect HIS image created in us.

What about a sexy soul of mind, will and emotions? It might be best to use it less in quantity and more in quality via a soulful song, a heart-felt talk and simply sharing honest opinions and encouraging goodwill among others. So, what is spiritually attractive? Virtue, is and can be read in the bible. Proverbs 31:1-31 In fact, the word "sexy" does not appear in the bible, although the nuance of it is indeed captured in the Songs of SONG OF Solomon one of the Books of Poetry in the of the Old Testament.

JOURNALIZE AND POLISH YOUR PURPOSE:

- We all have crossed paths with the latest product of sexiness... a juicy burger, a Heartfelt song, a leather covered book or even a sleek cell phone.
- **What is your definition of sexy and how would you use it to glorify God?**

23

SHE SAID YES! LIFE IS A SCREENPLAY
WJF – Ways to Make You Over!

INT. "The screenplay BOWLING ALLEY" A Décor of old fashioned romance and a nostalgic evening…
PLACES, EVERYONE!

INT. – (WRITTEN in Screenplay Style, Screenplay Bowling Alley – Early Evening
Eileen takes it all in as River gives history to the alley. Babe, we are inside the BOWLING ALLEY which features a decor of old fashioned romance, Wall photos of famous skaters and great food. Babe, here's to a nostalgic Evening)

Well River, as promised, I have all the ingredients of a great date complete with ugly shoes, a terrific anticipated cheeseburger and a host of some crazy yet wonderful people joining us your family.

Looks at her shoes in disbelief and tells River, Ugh, by the looks of these puppies, so far, you've kept your promise. Tomorrow, I must buy new shoes!

Great now let's go get that cheeseburger just ahead at the Karaoke dining area to order food.

River, "You are so funny! You brought me here an hour early to give me a rundown of your entire family. If they are as colorful and interesting as you say, I can't wait to meet them.

River, says great! Now, turn around. Here they come! Hello families ... meet Eileen. They encircle the lobby with well wishes.

RIVER
Alright Family, you have a lifetime to get to know Eileen, let's head over to the lanes.

Aunt LACARA
Children, you all have the gutter free bumper lanes. Enjoy!

Teen-agers and Adults, you have the regular open gutter bumper lanes!

They head for the lanes.

AUNT ALESHIA,
Attention Family, before we begin let's remind Gainer that we don't need bowling rule brochures...

Gainer
No problems as you are referring to Bowling Rule brochures? I don't have them. I DO have a few tips from "Bowling for Dummies!"

AUNT LACARA
Rocks her head side-to-side and exclaims, who are you calling a dummy? Girl, don't make me pull my earrings off. Here, I got petroleum jelly/grease in my pocket book!"

GAINER,
Don't get your panty bloomers in a bunch. These are merely Sift Notes.

FAMILY,
Who is he?

GAINER
(Puzzled, she starts rubbing her head.)
OMG! Sift notes are not people! it is an online reference site used for quick research on people, places and things!

SEAN,
Sorry, but that is incorrect Aunt Gainer. just described a NOUN!
FAMILY STARTS LAUGHING
FAMILY claps, you tell her Sean! That's my boy! Way to go Sean!

GAINER
Is so surprised by Sean's correction that she not only welcomed it, she praised him for it. She says, with much admiration, Thanks Sean.

Anyway, here is a tip for throwing the perfect shot which can lead to a higher bowling score; throwing lots of perfect shots can lead to a perfect game — a score of 300. To achieve a perfect hook shot:
POND,
Isn't that "HOOK SHOT" a swig of Vodka chased by a Colt 45 with lime?
LAKE,
Dude, what do you know about Shots and Chasers!?

INT. –SMOOTH RESIDENCE – EARLY AFTERNOON
POND,
Nothing much, other than Deacon Otto B. Smooth keeps his hidden under their flower stand when you walk in their foyer. He bought Girl Scout cookies from Milani one day. Ten boxes! We ran back to her wagon I was pulling with my bike.

Same here! Me too! He was looking for change to buy my candy from the basketball team. I had a pair of Sneakers under my arm. He said...

Deacon Otto B. Smooth

Hey boy, what are you doing with those new sneakers under your arm? You have a pair on, did you steal them?
LAKE
Of course not. I have outgrown this size 10, so I'm going to donate them to the church for the needy children's box. These were last year's make named after the famous Ohio Player.
DEACON OTTA B. SMOOTH
Sings, "Say what? Rollercoaster Child" "those over here, cause love going to be here!" I really like your style!

LAKE
Not those Ohio Players! Anyway, he was so happy that he bought four bars for ten dollars!

Mrs. Smooth
shouted from upstairs
Otto B., what are you doing down there?

(Singing under his breath, "I want to be Free by the Ohio Players).
LAKE
I took off.
MRS. SMOOTH
What did you do today?
(closes door) Deacon Smooth

(Two verses of Ohio players Skin Tight play said you're a bad, bad Mrs., In those skin-tight britches. Running folks in ditches. Skin TIGHT.)

INT. BACK TO BOWLING ALLEY – AFTERNOON
GAINER
Straighten the wrist of your bowling hand.
Your bowling hand, not surprisingly, is the one that's holding the ball. Be careful not to bend or flex your wrist.
Hold your hand straight while you swing the ball out and back.

BASS GRANDKIDS IN UNISON
Let go of the ball near your shoe,
Let the ball go and make a handshake too!
Your handshake should point up your thumb,
NOW, "Give me Five" BECAUSE we are having fun!

AUNT IRENE
As for scoring, the bowling alley keeps tally of the scores. have fun!
LIZ
Hello Eileen. It is such a pleasure to have you here. How is business at the florist SHOP?
EILEEN
It's great. Thank you for asking.
MG
By the way those mint chocolate candies you brought by the house were very good. Thank you so much.

EILEEN
You're welcome. They were samples. But now that I have someone with discriminating taste, I'll be sure to order a few boxes.

MG

Great! Call me as other samples arrive!

LIZ

MG!

RIVER

Be careful Eileen. You're treading dangerous waters in trying satisfying Dad's sweet tooth.

MG

What sweet tooth? I've got everything under control. (He grabs Liz's wheelchair). Come on honey let's go over to the Bowling Grill.

LIZ

What are we going for MG?

MG

What else? A chocolate milkshake!

RIVER

(NOTICES EILEEN RUBBING HER LEG) Eileen, how's your leg?

EILEEN

Oh, it's fine. I'll be bowling in no time!

RIVER

I think you should stay off it.

EILEEN

Now River don't start babying me. I'm fine. (THE FAMILY STARTS WALKING TOWARD THEM). Why are your family members walking toward us and smiling? Wait a minute, there's my Mom! Dad? Michelle too? Hey, there's the rest of my family! What are you all doing here?

FAMILY

Ask River!

EILEEN

River what is going on? Why are our families here?

RIVER

Probably so they won't miss out on this.

EILEEN

Miss out on what?

RIVER

I don't want them to miss out on the story about an angel that came into my life.

(THE SONG "THERE'S NO DISABILITY IN HER SWEET ENGAGING SMILE" start playing. FLASHES OF DIFFERENT VIRGINIA SCENES START SHOWING, for example Williamsburg Busch Gardens show, Doswell Kings Dominion train ride, The Portsmouth Aquarium, eating ice cream at Virginia Beach, watching the circus at The Hampton Coliseum, Ballet at Chesapeake where he falls asleep watching and she nudges him.

Eileen "Scrap Iron" Vasquez…

FAMILY

Scrap Iron?!

RIVER

…will you marry me?

EILEEN

Yes!

FAMILIES AND BOWLING ALLEY ASSOCIATES –

She said Yes!

Congratulations River & Eileen!

Song: True Love is an Action

Written by T. Cobb Morgan

8/18/2014 LizLL03@aol.com

You say you love me so but true love is an action

Heard you say this many time to no satisfaction.

L-O-V-E Love is what I'm dreaming of.

L-O-V-E Love is what I'm dreaming of.
Shoo doop, Shoop do, do, do!

You say you love me so but true love is an action
Heard you say this many times to no satisfaction.
L-O-V-E Love is what I'm dreaming of.
L-O-V-E Love is what I'm dreaming, dreaming of.
Shoo doop, Shoop do, do, do!
Show me love every day, that's all I have to say,
Your words are merely SUBTRACTIONS; I need to see it in your actions.

Song: True Love is an Action
Written by T. Cobb Morgan
8/18/2014 LizLL03@aol.com

Show me Love on a Sunday; Shake, Shake, Shake!
Show UP ON a Monday; My eyes are
wide awake!
Then on a Tuesday; My heart beat a double take!
Mid-week on a Wednesday; With one glance FROM THE start,
Kick it on a Thursday; My emotions in a million parts,
Chill on a Friday; My thoughts carried away in a cart,
True Love on a Saturday; PLEASE return my ransomed heart!
Show me love every day, that's all I have to say,
Your words are merely SUBTRACTIONS; I need to see it in your actions.
You say you love me so but true love is an action
Heard you say this many times to no satisfaction.
L-O-V-E Love is what I'm dreaming of.

L-O-V-E Love is what I'm dreaming of.
Shoo doop, Shoop do, do, do!

You say you love me so but true love is an action
Heard you say this many times to no satisfaction.
L-O-V-E Love is what I'm dreaming of.
L-O-V-E Love is what I'm dreaming, dreaming of.
Shoo doop, Shoop do, do, do!

Love is an Action
Written by T. Cobb Morgan
8/18/2014 LizLL03@aol.com

STOP! To Work on WJF: Worksheet, Journal REFLECT & FOCUS at the end of each chapter or CONTINUE.

Manifestation end of Chapter Twenty-Three, She said Yes, Life is a Screenplay WJF, Ways to Make ME OVER!

<u>PRAYER</u>: Pray for 26 seconds on Topic of Focus - **Biblical Manifestation: Ways to make you Over**

<u>DEVOTION</u>: Take twenty-six (26) minutes to read chapter and challenge

W – WAYS TO MAKE Me OVER
Galatians 3:26 For you are all sons of God through faith in Christ Jesus.

1 Peter 1:23 for you have been born again not of seed which is perishable but Imperishable, that
is, through the living and enduring word of God.

JOURNAL: HOW WOULD YOU LIKE TO BE SPIRITUALLY MADE OVER?

FISH QUOTE:

To reinvent yourself on the outside
Make sure that new look will do
God created you in his image a creation just for you
the best way to make yourself over
is to look carefully inside,
Ask yourself honestly what is there to
improve or maybe what is there to hide?
T. COBB-MORGAN

24

HOW TO LIVE YOUR FAITH-BASED LIFE TO YOUR FULL POTENTIAL IN 26 DAYS!
WJF - Ways to Make You Smarter

FADE IN

INT. EILEEN'S CONDO-EARLY MORNING

DORIS (EILEEN'S MOM)

I LIKE RIVER; HE's a very nice man.
Eileen, have you had a chance to think about the wedding plans.

Eileen responds, Yes, mom, I would like Velicia, my sister-in-law to plan my wedding after I speak with River. I'd like to keep the budget low and the guest list small and intimate. Great food, entertainment and guests gathered around the gazebo arch at Fort Monroe, Virginia. Then after a short honeymoon celebration at the hot springs resort, we will come back home. I don't want to close the shop too long.

Dori, adds Shop? Why not sell the shop and work on my grandchildren and come to California!

Eileen explains, Mom, I don't want to lose "me" in this marriage. I enjoy my independence and keeping my business prosperous! Besides, I must help Michael send Michelle to college next year. I promised Trina on her deathbed and I'm looking forward to it. She's my daughter.

Dori speaks, I know baby. I'm sorry for being selfish. Go to bed and get some rest. By the way, what are you reading?

Rev. Sandra Penney gave River and me some pre-counseling literature to read before we get married. Liz was one of her speakers and she shared her screenplay and book:

From the Chronicles of I Thank God that Big Mouth Bass Don't Talk, or Do They? Features, How to Live your Faith-Based Life to your Full Potential and Purpose in 26 Days! 0 THANK GOD THAT BIG MOUTH BASS DON'T TALK, OR DO THEY?
Also included is My Beautiful Noir Madonna, Speaks Healing in the Spoken Word.
Dori, Child Speak to Me!
Well Mom in her SERIES I she speaks on:
KNEEL and Ask God "Why?" Five Steps to
HEAL Your Broken, Ugly, Leaking Life and
REVEAL Your Five Purposes!
SEAL a Smarter, Sexier, Saner, Savvy and Successful You!

REVEAL Five Easy Steps to understand our purpose. They are found in the Holy Bible in Romans 5: 1-5. We are to glory in our suffering because suffering produces perseverance; perseverance, character; and character, hope. Hope with God's love, reveals our purpose and opens doors.

We are here on earth with five purposes to fulfill. Your first purpose is the first commandment, Matthew 22: 34-38. It reads: But when the Pharisees heard that he had silenced the Sadducees, they gathered together. 35 And one of them, a lawyer, asked him a question to test him:

Teacher, which is the great commandment in the Law?" 37 And he said to him, "You shall love the Lord your God with all your heart and with all your soul and with YOUR ENTIRE mind. 38 This is the great and first commandment.

Your SECOND PURPOSE - The Second Commandment) is Matthew 22; 39-40 - Honoring Our Second Greatest Purpose. You shall love your neighbor (others) as yourself.

Your Third Purpose - The Great Commission Matthew 28: 16-20

16 Now the eleven disciples went to Galilee, to the mountain to which Jesus had directed them. 17 And when they saw him they worshiped him, but some doubted. 18 And Jesus came and said to them, "All authority in heaven and on earth has been given to me. 19 Go therefore and make disciples of all nations, baptizing them in[b] the name of the Father and of the Son and of the Holy Spirit, 20 teaching them to observe all that I have commanded you. And behold, I am with you always, to the end of the age."

Finally, we are to glorify God with our fourth purpose, spiritual gifts and fifth purpose, natural talents.

As a refresher, she invited the couples to split up and share which wife chose the key word Smart, Sexy, Sane, SAVVY AND Successful. They are all described in the "Virtuous Woman" biblical passage of Proverbs.

DORIS, Whew, sounds like work! If your Dad and I had gone through that training we might still be together.

EILEEN sighs, Goodnight Mom.

She reads, "The Virtuous Woman"-Proverbs 31:10-31 (KJV Bible)

[10] Who can find a virtuous woman? for her price is far above rubies. (Successful)

[11] The heart of her husband doth safely trust in her, so that he shall have no need of spoil. (Smart) [12] She will do him good and not evil all the days of her life. (Sexy)

[13] She seeketh wool, and flax, and worketh willingly with her hands. (Savvy)

[14] She is like the merchants' ships; she bringeth her food from afar. (Savvy)

[15] She riseth also while it is yet night, and giveth meat to her household, and a portion to her maidens. (Smart)

[16] She considereth a field, and buyeth it: with the fruit of her hands she planteth a vineyard. (Smart)

[17] She girdeth her loins with strength, and strengthened her arms. (Sexy)

[18] She perceiveth that her merchandise is good: her candle goeth not out by night. (Smart)

[19] She layeth her hands to the spindle, and her hands hold the distaff. (Savvy)

[20] She stretcheth out her hand to the poor; yea, she reacheth forth her hands to the needy.

[21] She is not afraid of the snow for her household: for all her household are clothed with scarlet.

[22] She maketh herself coverings of tapestry; her clothing is silk and purple.

[23] Her husband is known in the gates, when he sitteth among the elders of the land. (Sane)

[24] She maketh fine linen, and selleth it; and delivereth girdles unto the merchant.

[25] Strength and honor are her clothing; and she shall rejoice in time to come. (Sane)

[26] She openeth her mouth with wisdom; and in her tongue, is the law of kindness. (Smart)

[27] She looketh well to the ways of her household, and eateth not the bread of idleness. (Savvy)

²⁸ Her children arise up, and call her blessed; her husband also, and he praiseth her.

²⁹ Many daughters have done virtuously, but thou excellest them all (Successful). ³⁰ Favor is deceitful, and beauty is vain: but a woman that feareth the LORD, she shall be praised. ³¹ Give her of the fruit of her hands; let her own works praise her in the gates

God, thank you for insight and wisdom. I love you Lord, good-night.

STOP! To Work on WJF: Worksheet, Journal REFLECT & FOCUS at the end of each chapter or CONTINUE.

Manifestation end of
Chapter Twenty-Four
HOW TO LIVE YOUR FAITH BASED
IFE TO YOUR FULL POTENTIAL
IN 26 DAYS –

WJF - Ways to make you smarter!

PRAYER: Pray for 26 seconds on Topic of Focus - **Biblical Manifestation: ways to make you smarter**

DEVOTION: Take 26 minutes to read chapter and challenge

W – WAYS TO MAKE YOU SMARTER

[26] Brothers and sisters, think of what you were when you were called. Not many of you were wise by human standards; not many were influential; not many were of noble birth. [27] But God chose the foolish things of the world to shame the wise; God chose the weak things of the world to shame the strong. [28] God chose the lowly things of this world and the despised things—and the things that are not—to nullify the things that are, [29] so that no one may boast before him. [30] It is because of him that you are in Christ Jesus, who has become for us wisdom from God—that is, our righteousness, holiness and redemption. [31] Therefore, as it is written: "Let the one who boasts boast in the Lord." [I Corinthians 1: 26- 31]

Here is a list beneficial to you according to the Bible to make you smarter; these are also ways God speaks to us.

1. Listen,
2. Look at nature

3. Learn from your mistakes
4. Read everything in the Bible!
5. Believe and help someone else to achieve.
6. Learn a new skill or hobby
7. Examine the quality of your relationship and friendship
8. Take care of yourself.
9. Cry a good physical, spiritual and soul cleansing cry.
10. Laugh out loud!

JOURNALIZE: List more things to make you smarter.

Add a list of ten Additional items to buddy challenge a friend to try with you on the 26-day plan to make you smarter.

12.

13.

14.

15.

16,

17.

18.

19

20

FISH QUOTE: THE SMARTEST THING YOU CAN DO IN THE BIBLE IS TO READ IT. T. COBB-MORGAN

25

GET UP IT'S TIME FOR CHURCH!
WJF – Polish Your Purpose

INT. ZION PROSPECT Baptist CHURCH – MORNING SERVICE SIX MONTHS LATER
(CHOIR FINISHING SONG, "The Lord is My Strength and Song" taken from Exodus 15:2, 3 & 11)

2 The LORD is my strength and song, and he is become my salvation: he is my God, and I will prepare him a habitation; my father's God, and I will exalt him.

11 Who is like unto thee, O LORD, among the gods? who is like thee, glorious in holiness, fearful in praises, doing wonders?

Choir Director (Directs Choir to sit down)

PASTOR proceeds to the pulpit and the audience stands. Good Morning Church. Please open your bible to the book of Joshua

Joshua 1 The LORD Commissions Joshua

1 After Moses the LORD's servant died, the LORD said to Joshua son of Nun, Moses' assistant: 2 "Moses my servant is dead. Get ready! Cross the

Jordan River! Lead these people into the land which I am ready to hand over to them. ³ I am handing over to you every place you set foot, as I promised Moses. ⁴ Your territory will extend from the wilderness in the south to Lebanon in the north. It will extend all the way to the great River Euphrates in the east (including all of Syria) and all the way to the Mediterranean Sea in the west. ⁵ No one will be able to resist you all the days of your life.

MG, whispers, Take your time Liz. MG slowly strolls Liz down the aisle to front bench of the church. Liz looks over and sees Muhammed Ali's (another Parkinson's Survivor who just passed away) daughter, Laila holding up her fist as if to say, stay strong Liz!

As I was with Moses, so I will be with you. I will not abandon you or leave you alone. ⁶ Be strong and brave! You must lead these people in the conquest of this land that I solemnly promised their ancestors I would hand over to them. ⁷ Make sure you are very strong and brave! Carefully obey all the law my servant Moses charged you to keep! Do not swerve from it to the right or to the left, so that you may be successful in all you do. ⁸ This law scroll must not leave your lips!

PASTOR CONT'D

So, you see, Sister Liz, you must memorize it day and night so you can carefully obey all that is written in it. Then you will prosper and be successful as evident with your screenplay. ⁹ I repeat, be strong and brave! Don't be afraid and don't panic, for I, the LORD your God, am with you in all you do."

PASTOR CONT" D

By the way, the Board of Trustees and I thank you for your tithes and generous offering. Any witnesses in here?

Grannie Hog Maw

...Amen Pastor, because Salvation is free but everything else cost! (audience laughs) Snort, Snort, what the smell?

RIVER, sees his mother showing her full face) Mom?

LIZ, (Whisper) Hello River.

RIVER

Good Morning Church. This next song, is my personal testimony. My mother told me that when you encounter suffering in your life whether it be an injury, illness or disease…ask God why? Through your faith, he will reveal your purpose. As proof, she directed me to Romans 5:1-5 for the Five principles. Therefore, since we have been justified by faith, we have peace with God through our Lord Jesus Christ. Through him we have also obtained access by faith into this grace in which we stand, and we rejoice in hope of the glory of God. More than that, we rejoice in our sufferings, knowing that suffering produces endurance, and endurance produces character, and character produces hope, and hope does not put us to shame, with God's love.

Crossing the Jordan River
Written by Terry Morgan
Pond sings as little RJ: Sings I got Joy like a river in my soul.
Grandma: Good job RJ!
Pond sings as little RJ: Thank you Grandma.
River: I can hear my Grandma say…
Hook: Ash, He crossed the Jordan River, Ahhh, He did it for you and me,
Ahhh, Joshua walked on dry ground, Ahhh, for the whole world to see

Hook and Verse:

Ahhh, He crossed the Jordan River, (Joshua's camp got up early one morning)
Ahhh, He did it for you and me, (As soon as you see the Ark of the promise)

Ahhh, Joshua walked on dry ground, (Break camp and follow them)
Ahhh, for the whole world to see!

Hook and Verse:

Ahhh, He crossed the Jordan River, (Joshua received honor)
Ahhh, He did it for you and me, (As a sign He is with us as with Moses)
Ahhh, Joshua walked on dry ground, (When you step into the Jordan, <u>stand</u>)
Ahhh, for the whole world to see!
Ahhh, He crossed the Jordan River, (They chose among the 12 tribes)
Ahhh, He did it for you and me, (The river stopped flowing and stood up like a dam!)
Ahhh, Joshua walked on dry ground, (The whole nation stood on dry ground)
Ahhh, for the whole world to see!

Ahhh, He crossed the Jordan River, (To those crossing a Jordan River in your life)
Ahhh, He did it for you and me, (He will still do it for you and me)
Ahhh, Joshua walked on dry ground, (And place you on dry ground)
Ahhh, for the whole world to see!

Closing Hook:

Ahhh, He crossed the Jordan River, (John the Baptist felt unworthy to baptize Jesus)

Ahhh, He did it for you and me, (Because Jesus was sinless)
Ahhh, Joshua walked on dry ground, (but He to fulfill all righteousness)
Ahhh, for the whole world to see!

GOD SAID THIS I MY BELOVED SON IN WHOM I AM WELL PLEASED!

Ahhh, He crossed the Jordan River, Ahhh, He did it for you and me,
Ahhh, Joshua walked on dry ground, Ahhh, for the whole world to see!
(written by Terry Morgan /11/2014)
LIZ, SAYS HE AROSE THIS EASTER MORNING. AND WHEN HE DID, SO DID I!

PASTOR
May the Church say AMEN.
CHURCH: amen! FADE OUT

STOP! To Work on WJF: Worksheet, Journal REFLECT & FOCUS at the end of each chapter or CONTINUE.

Manifestation end of
Chapter Twenty-five
"get up, it is time for church"
WJF – Polish your purpose!

PRAYER: Pray for 26 seconds on Topic of Focus - **Biblical Manifestation: Polish Your Purpose time for church**

DEVOTION: Take 26 minutes to read chapter and challenge question.

P – POLISH YOUR PURPOSE!
26 This *is* the purpose that is purposed upon the whole earth: and this *is* the hand that is stretched out upon all the nations.
27 For the LORD of hosts hath purposed, and who shall disannul *it*? and his hand *is* stretched out, and who shall turn it back? Isaiah 14:26-27

Journal - polish your purpose!

Question: What does it mean to polish your purpose?

Answer: To desire an awareness to raise the bar and heighten your spirit of excellence for your fivefold purpose 1. Love the Lord, 2 To Love Your Neighbor, 3 Be Fishers of Man and 4glorify God with your spiritual Gifts (you receive after salvation) and 5 praise him with your natural Talents.

add your Definition of Polish:

1. To make smooth and shiny.
2. To refine or remove flaws from; perfect or complete: *polish one's piano technique; polish up the*
4. Elegance of style or manners; refinement.
5. Yours-

FISH QUOTE: POLISH YOUR PURPOSE WHEN YOU SEEK THE WISDOM OF THE LIGHT,
AND WISDOM OF PURPOSE WILL POLISH LIGHT AT NIGHT.

26

SOUND THE WEDDING BELLS
LOVE IS AN ACTION
WJF - Quit Now? Be Steadfast Your
Break through is Around the Corner

FADE IN
EXT. FORT MONROE, VA - AFTERNOON

EILEEN's eyes fill with tears as she looks around the wedding Gazebo decorated in tiny blue and yellow roses with white bluebells she made this past week. The Matron of Honor chair reserved for her best friend Katrina's gorgeous Maui bouquet. Their daughter Michelle, Maid of Honor, will be seated at the opposite position.

What a beautiful day here at Fort Monroe for wedding celebration! River, what are you most thankful for to God?

"Coffee," he says. Why coffee? Eileen asks. River pulls up to the café table and proceeds with his story. One day my mom asked me what was troubling me. I told her nothing. She replied, don't lie to me boy. However, I love you too much to get angry for not sharing. Just like your Grandma Sarah, you love coffee. So, every morning you have coffee, have coffee with God. Even if you only have time for the shortest prayer, "Which is Thanks."

Eileen smiles, sounds just like Mama Liz. Yes, this is a true funny story and this is the funniest part. Grandma Sarah had just finished brewing a fresh pot of coffee and she was out of sugar. Her devotion that morning was in 1 Thessalonians 5:18, King James Version, [18] in everything give thanks; for this is the will of God in Christ Jesus for you. As she was finishing her prayer, my Uncle June, then nine (9) months old, was crying. Grandma Sarah decided to quickly change his diaper. Immediately pee squirted everywhere and a few drops sprinkled in her coffee!

Eileen asked, oh no, what did she do?

River, chuckled, instead of getting upset, she smiled, looked up and said Lord, thank you for the sweetener. She was so wise. She knew that all blessings come from God. Oh, and she also knew that whether you have a cup of coffee, a glass of water off tap or the most expensive champagne in France… it all comes out pee!

Eileen, grinning, River, you are too funny! What's that in your hand?

River hands her a hanky. This is for my beautiful bride. (He gives her a freshly starched but old linen hanky with blue belle flowers.) My grandmother would want you to have "something blue"- blue bells were her favorite.

Kelicia comes over. Excuse me you two lovebirds, but I need the bride quickly to change. Oh, River this box arrived for you.

River responds thanks! (He curiously opens the note inside box and it read) Dear River Here is "The Light" you were drawn to in the river rock. The sunlight reflected fifteen **gold coins encrusted with diamonds wedged between two river boulders! (Appears to be the authentic coins of King TerLyndoso dowry to his daughter to pay for her services in America back in 1420. It was a tiny ivory box encased in animal skin and bordered with animal teeth a symbol of "sheer grit and grind courage." Wedding blessings, Pink Lady."**

(He looks up to Heaven and says tearfully)

Oh, thank you God for being so wise, timely, generous and loving to our family. This will buy quite a few ramps for the "Wheelchair Rollin' Kids and Elderly Bizz" benefit!

Aunt Aleshia.

Gather around everybody! Where is Reverend Sandra Penney?

REVEREND PENNY plans for officiating, yells, Here I am!

Aunt Irene asks, where is River and Eileen?

Kelicia/ wedding planner, places, EVERYONE! All family, friends and special guests please take your positions. No assembly once the ceremony begins. Thank you.

Grandmother Tootsie, May God Bless Marriage Because One Day you'll wake up broken, feeling ugly and the leaking won't stop!

My Dear River and Eileen,

May today be one of your many joyous celebrations,

Thanking God for His divine love and sweet adoration.

Always remember your love brought you here for this special occasion,

Not fate, nor circumstances, nor even insincere persuasion,

So, don't try to figure it all out as you go along,

Just remember to have fun as you both right your wrongs

Yes, you might break each other's heart as you meander this matrimonial course,

The secret is to say you're sorry with genuine and honest remorse.

Live, Love, laugh so hard until you roll on the floor,

And there will be days you'll wish to be out of the door!

Ask each other for forgiveness and try hard to be true and kind,

As you build a home, raise your family and come home to unwind.

One day you'll wake up broken, ugly and the leaking won't stop!
You'd better think fast; hold it together, toss out the mirror and grab a mop!
Read Romans 5:1-5 those five easy steps,
Have Faith, glorify suffering, Perseverance, character, And HOPE & love God to stay blessed!
Because the years will go by so fast; today you're young but to-morrow you'll be old,
But not one day of marriage would you trade for all life's trea-sures of silver and gold.
Written by Terry Morgan –

KELICIA
River, you may begin.
RIVER
SINGS SONG
Processional Begins:
BEST MAN
MATRON OF HONOR
GROOMSMEN
BRIDESMAIDS
FLOWER GIRL
RING BEARER

FATHER-OF-THE-BRIDE
Sweetheart, are you sure you want to do this?
BRIDE
Yes Daddy, I want to walk the aisle without my chair.
FATHER-OF-THE-BRIDE
Very well. Hold on to my arm and relax. Take your time.
They proceed down the aisle.

RIVER
Starts singing song.
SONG: "There's No Disability in Her Sweet Engaging Smile"
(Verse): Let me tell you about an angel that came into my life,
She shook my whole world up; calmed my toils and strife.
Life dealt her disabilities, yet she moved with grace and style.
(Hook): And when she turned around, found my wife to wed the aisle.
There's no disability in her sweet engaging smile.
She stole my heart, (Her smile)
She stole my mind, (Her smile)
She stole my love, (Her smile)
...And now she's mine.
(Hook): And when she turned around...found my wife to wed the aisle.
There's no disability in her sweet engaging smile.
(Verse): I can't understand how she makes it through the day.
Her body wrapped in pain, yet she always makes a way.
When she looks in my eyes, I know that I belong,
She dances on my heart, my soul she sings a song.
(Hook): And when she turned around ...found my wife to wed the aisle
There's no disability in her sweet engaging smile.
She stole my heart, (Her smile)
She stole my mind, (Her smile)
She stole my love, (Her smile)
...And now she's mine.
(Hook): And when she turned around ...found my wife to wed the aisle.
There's no disability in her sweet engaging smile.
She stole my heart, (Her smile)

She stole my mind, (Her smile)
She stole my love, (Her smile)
…And now she's mine.
And when she turned around …found my wife to wed the aisle,
There's no disability in her sweet engaging smile.

T. Cobb Morgan: LizLL03@aol.com

REVEREND

Do you, River, and you, Eileen take each other through this this spiritual journey of love, respect, AND FAITH, HOPE, blessed to be called marriage?

RIVER AND EILEEN

(In unison) We do absolutely! (They Kiss). Eileen throws the bouquet. All the aunts crowd up front and Aunt Irene catches it!

Grannie Hog Ma

LOOKING INTO CAMERA

Snort, Snort, What the Smell?! AM I ON T.V.? Testing. Well, there's two ways to look at this. The bad news is I didn't catch the "BRULEE" (bouquet) because Penelope Pig Pen boxed me out with her "PaDonka Donk! But, the good news is I'm still single! (She winks at the camera)

MUSIC STARTS! LOVE IS AN ACTION

STOP! To Work on WJF: Worksheet, Journal REFLECT & FOCUS at the end of each chapter or CONTINUE.

MANIFESTATION: Q - qUIT nOW? bE sTEADFAST YOUR BREAKTHROUGH IS AROUND THE CORNER.
PRAYER: PRAY FOR TWENTY-SIX SECONDS TO RENEW, RE-FRESH, REBUILD AND RESTORE.

DEVOTION: TAKE 26 MINUTES FOR READING ISAIAH 26:3 YOU WILL KEEP IN PEACE WHOSE MIND STAYS STEADFAST BECAUSE THEY TRUST YOU.
James, a servant of God and of the Lord Jesus Christ, To the twelve tribes in the Dispersion: Greetings. Count it all joy, my brothers, when you meet trials of various kinds, for you know that the testing of your faith produces steadfastness. And let steadfastness have its full effect, that you may be perfect and complete, lacking in nothing. If any of you lacks wisdom, let him ask God, who gives generously to all without reproach, and it will be given him. ... **James 1:1-6**
STRETCH IN BED, DO TOE TOUCHES ON THE TOILET, HAVE BREAKFAST, SHOWER, SHAVE, ON RIDE TO WORK. YOU MAY ALSO FORM A LUNCH, CHURCH OR SUNDAY SCHOOL STUDY GROUP TO REVIEW A CHAPTER EACH DAY.
jOURNALIZE: a recent breakthrough

HOOK QUOTE:

LIFE IS FOR THE LIVING, TAKE A WALK ALONG THE SHORE,
THANKS FOR ALL THAT'S BEEN GIVEN, IN HIS NAME, BLESSINGS GALORE.

PICK UP SHELLS, SMELL THE SALTY AIR, GUIDE A TURTLE BACK TO SEA,
YOU BOTH WALK SLOWLY TAKING IN ALL THE BEAUTY NATURE OFFERS FOR FREE. T. COBB-MORGAN

THE MOVIE TRAILER FOR:
"I THANK GOD THAT BIG MOUTH BASS DON'T TALK, OR
DO THEY?"

They say Virginia is for Lovers,

...Especially on a relaxing day, quiet enjoyment on the river and the bass fish are biting. Too quiet? Well, if you're looking for a little more excitement...

Then run!

to this next movie, Blockbuster that is. Meet the superstar studded family cast, The Bass Family that is if you're looking up at the sky!

Then look down at this unspoiled, home grown family and cast worthy crop!

If you look in the Family Album,

You're sure to see the Bass Group,
Most people have one inner child, but River has two;

THERE'S POND, River's 7 yr. old inner child.
And Lake, River's 17 yr. Old inner child.

Now meet River. You say, "Who is River"

Well, he's the star of the show! He's got four women in his ear. What is a man to do? He needs to be four men!

First there is his mom, LIZ; SHE is an amazing Parkinson's survivor. One day she heard River sing in the shower and wrote this screenplay and soundtrack... in bed!

As a voice of advocacy for disabled individuals to live their lives to the fullest, she battles her own fears and the rest is history! Her husband, MG, hasn't slept since!

I need a recliner, lemon water a nap!

Then there is my Ex-fiancée Delilah, who traded him for HIS BEST friend Larkson...

"Snort, Snort WHAT THE smell?! Is this microphone on? Forget the crazy ex-girlfriend, that's my spot she's in! I'm Grannie Hog Ma and we are going to have a wild crazy ride!"

Snort, SNORT, "What the Smell?" – Y'all get ready for snuff dipping, joy juice sipping, smart mouth lipping but I ain't tripping, so you better get outta my face and get to skipping or rumble with my Grannie Hog Ma shuffle and catch a butt Whipping! Oh, God bless you Sugar!

Did I mention meeting Eileen, his true love, and six months later under "friendly fire" only to dig up a ten-year-old "hostile fire" secret from his military past!

Being a self-professed gummi worm sports angler, please meet the other woman in his life ...Big Mouth Pink Lady Sassy BASS!

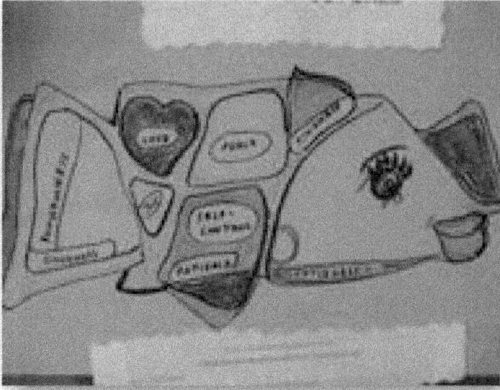

PINK LADY. SHE IS River's animated spiritual advisor and confidant.

Who are you calling big mouth?

Not one to gossip, cause you show ain't not heard it from me.

But have you *met* River's family? Those Aunts (Spicy, well-seasoned, "Round the Way" WOMEN. shall WE MENTION the remaining members?

AUNT IRENE: ASKS, RIVER are you bouncing at your club tonight? I Want to check out the 80-yr. old's. You know the ones with one foot in the grave...on the other hand ... MY ARTHRITIS will send me home for a nap!

AUNT ALESHIA…one on a banana peel! Look girl, you'd better

Join me in the cougar trot!
after MY NAP!

Gee. I don't know whether to BRING BYOB, a tonic kicker or Baby Formula! THEIR NAPS ARE RUINING messing with my pyt vibes!
AUNT LACARA

AUNT GAINER aka Dr. Gainer – My sisters are hilarious and…

Whisper: But, my professional opinion? They ALL need therapy.

Do I smell fish frying?

LAKE
Oh no. this can't be good.

(AUNT IRENE's CAT walks by burping and stomach appears very bloated.)

Come join them for a delicious soul fool dinner.
    and, for dessert we have...

HEAD BURGLAR

...Oh no, a stick up! Everybody hands up!

A/C

That's right we are the a/c bandits. We serviced your air conditioner and came back to rob you!

HEAD BURGLAR

Just shut up! Miriam, stop talking!

FAMILY

Miriam?!

Oh, DID I mention the Bad Bass grandkids? Amazing what these kids can do with hot water balloons and cayenne pepper!

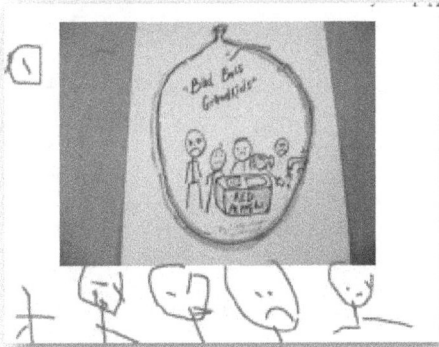

NARRATOR
How about we turn in for a quiet night cap of?
FAMIY

"SPADES" Yes, a game of Spades sounds good! We are in, Get the cards.
Don't stay up too late, BECAUSE tomorrow morning we are having...

NARRATOR:
Church!

www.ingramcontent.com/pod-product-compliance
Lightning Source LLC
LaVergne TN
LVHW051227080426
835513LV00016B/1450